A Voice from Harper's Ferry

Osborne P. Anderson

with essays by

Mumia Abu-Jamal
Vince Copeland
Monica Moorehead

World View Forum 📖 New York

A Voice from Harper's Ferry

ISBN 0-89567-136-0

Published and distributed by:

World View Forum
55 West 17th Street
New York, NY 10011

Phone (212) 627-2994
Fax (212) 675-7869
Email ww@wwpublish.com
Web http://www.workers.org

Available at discounted bulk rates for educational use. To place CREDIT CARD orders or for bookstore and university invoice orders and discounts, call 800-247-6553, 24-hour service, seven days a week.

Edited by Deirdre Griswold
Cover design by Lal Roohk

ABOUT THIS BOOK . . .

Osborne P. Anderson's account of the raid on Harper's Ferry appeared in pamphlet form in 1861 right after the start of the Civil War. However, it was not set in print again until 1974. In that year Vince Copeland, whose introduction "The Unfinished Revolution" is included in this book, rescued it from oblivion. A second printing appeared in 1980.

This third modern printing also includes contributions from Mumia Abu-Jamal and Monica Moorehead. Abu-Jamal has become known around the world for exposing racist police brutality and the prison system in the United States. He has done it from his jail cell, for he is presently on Death Row in Pennsylvania. A former Black Panther, a writer and radio journalist in Philadelphia, Abu-Jamal has become known as the "Voice of the Voiceless," much as Osborne Anderson was in his day.

Monica Moorehead is an organizer and fighter for Black liberation who was also the 1996 presidential candidate of Workers World Party. She has interviewed death row prisoners, including Mumia Abu-Jamal, in Texas and Pennsylvania. A former schoolteacher who took on the racist military establishment in Norfolk, Virginia, Moorehead has visited South Africa at the invitation of the African National Congress.

Contents

Acknowledgments

This book owes its existence to the voluntary sacrifice of many people. First came the commitment of Osborne P. Anderson, John Brown, and all their comrades to risk everything in the anti-slavery struggle. Only a handful survived. Most gave their lives, not for any material reward, but for an end to that cruel and hated system.

Other sacrifices may seem pale by comparison with giving one's life. But in any battle, there must be hundreds of supporters doing all the necessary backup work to sustain those on the front lines. Anderson's words would not have reached us today had there not been abolitionist printers, proofreaders, and distributors back in 1861. They too should be acknowledged.

Vince Copeland discovered Anderson's manuscript and first reprinted it in 1974, with the introduction included here.

Deirdre Griswold edited and typeset the present edition of this book. Lal Roohk designed the cover and searched for historical illustrations. Paddy Colligan proofread the final pages and checked the contents for accuracy. Sara Flounders assisted in the production process. Kathy Durkin coordinated the fundraising. Gary Wilson kept the computer network running. Sharon Ayling, Marsha Goldberg, and Scott Scheffer coordinated prepublication publicity.

Many people generously contributed to help pay for the book's publication. They are, in alphabetical order:

Pam Africa, International Concerned Family and Friends of Mumia Abu-Jamal; Dr. Bob Allen and family; Sharon Ayling; Susan Bailey; Lydia Bayoneta and Gene Clancy; Nick Camerota; Ellen Catalinotto; John Catalinotto; Ed Childs; Pat Chin in memory of Luvenia Pinson; Franco Ciabattoni; Cynthia Copeland Cochran; Hillel Cohen; Naomi Cohen, Fred Goldstein, and Lila Natalie Goldstein; Bill Covington; Bill Doares; Rachel Duell and John Jones; Kathy Durkin; Harvey "Tee" Earvin, Texas death row prison activist; Sharon Eolis in memory of Dorothy Ballan.

Also, Leslie Feinberg and Minnie Bruce Pratt; Irving Fierstein; Sherry Finkelman and Gavrielle Gemma; Sara Flounders; Mairead Skehan Gillis; Deirdre Griswold in memory of Elizabeth Ross Copeland; Joan Hamilton; Sue Harris and Janet Mayes; Imani Henry; Patricia Hilliard; Michelle Jacobsen-Da-Kadu; Marie Jay; a friend in memory of Beth Katz; Ziggy Klein; Michael Kramer; Cheryl Labash in memory of Wendell Phillips Addington; Phyllis Lucero; Joanie Marquardt; Key Martin in memory of Dorothy Martin; Beth Massey and Bill Massey.

Also, Bob McCubbin; Jeanette Merrill and Edward Merrill; David V. Morris for Adam Abdul Hakeem (Larry Davis); Lyn Neeley; Frank Neisser; Henri Nereaux; People's Video Network, Chris Hani Viva!; Mary Owen in memory of Susan Steinman; Cornelia Rakow and Ray Rakow; Lal Roohk and Gary Wilson; Art Rosen; Bill Sacks, Katy Rosen, Emma Sacks, and Malcolm Sacks; Gary Schaefer; Deirdre Sinnott; Al Strasburger; Phil Wilayto, A Job is a Right Campaign, Milwaukee, Wisconsin.

Also, the following branches of Workers World Party: Atlanta members and supporters; Baltimore; Boston, in memory of Henry Cohen, Danton Perez, Jane Polley, Bill Wycoff, and Marshall Yates; Buffalo, in memory of our dear comrades Vera Spruill and Ernestine Robinson, who were taken from us far too soon; Chicago; Cleveland; Houston; Los Angeles; Michigan; Philadelphia, in memory of Ray Ceci and Rosemarie Hill; Richmond; San Francisco; Washington, D.C.; and from the entire Party in memory of Dorothy Ballan, Vince Copeland, and Sam Marcy.

The neglected voices from Harper's Ferry

By Mumia Abu-Jamal

"Our brethren of the South should not be called slaves, but prisoners of war."
Robert Johnson, at a Boston protest of the hated Fugitive Slave law (from *Liberator*, 10 December 1852)

"History," the revered revolutionary Malcolm X advised, "best rewards our research." I thought of his words as I read Osborne P. Anderson's first-person account of the attack upon Harper's Ferry, Virginia, by the legendary John Brown and his small crew of armed supporters, on 17 October 1859.

The name of Osborne P. Anderson is virtually unknown, and as a participant in one of the most remarkable anti-slavery actions of its era, his account should be seen as an historical gold mine. Not only is his work virtually unknown, it remains virtually ignored. It is a measure of our historical myopia that his name is unknown and, perhaps more importantly, that his account, that of a Black revolutionary who fought for his people's freedom, is not known. His easy-to-read account opens the door to a history seldom seen.

Shortly before reading *A Voice from Harper's Ferry*, I read what is regarded as one of the "finest one-volume chronicles" of the U.S. Civil War (according to the *Wall Street Journal* blurb on the cover), James M. McPherson's *Battle Cry of Freedom: The Civil War Era*. Although his Pulitzer Prize-winning text is well written and flush with footnotes citing a wealth of sources, it presents a far different picture of the Harper's Ferry "raid," and of Brown's raiders. McPherson paints the picture of a Brown who is driven by a leaden sense of fatalism, and suggests the very notion of fomenting insurrection in the South was "strange," if not "apparently insane."[1] Anderson's account informs us that the action was influenced by the very real danger of detection by neighbors of the Washington County, Maryland, farmhouse where the men were training and assembling arms, and the delay of reinforcements from other areas:

> Not being satisfied as to the real business of "J. Smith & Sons" [Brown's *nom de guerre*—M.A.-J.] after that, and learning that several thousand stand of arms were to be removed by the Government from the Armory to some other point, threats to search the premises were made against the encampment. A tried friend having *given* information of *the state of public feeling* without, and of the intended process, *Captain Brown and party concluded to strike a blow immediately, and not*, as at first intended, *to await certain reinforcements* from the North and East, which would have been in Maryland within one and three weeks. Could other parties, waiting for the word, have reached headquarters in time for the outbreak when it took place, the taking of the armory, engine house, and rifle factory, would have been quite different. [Emphasis added]

Anderson, as an African in the Americas (he lived for a time in Chatham in Ontario), saw the wiry "Osawatomie Brown" as a kind of Moses, who was "chosen by God to this great work." "This great work" was the liberation of oppressed, and the establishment, if successful, of a new nation founded on freedom, not slavery.

Anderson was present and active at the Provisional Constitutional Convention held at Chatham, a free Black community of refugees from Yankee bondage, where a Constitution was adopted "for the proscribed and oppressed people 'of the United States of America.'" Officers of the Provisional Government, members of Congress, and Secretary of State were elected at the convention. Anderson himself was named to Congress.

While McPherson devotes several lines to Chatham, Anderson's invaluable account is not cited, and his name doesn't appear in the text, the footnotes, nor the index. It would have invaluably enriched his account, and given a unique perspective that is often missing from "history." For example, McPherson paints a picture of Black

---

[1] James M. McPherson, *Battle Cry of Freedom: The Civil War Era* (New York: Ballantine, 1988), 206, 208.

betrayal of Brown, and quotes a Black recruit from Cleveland who failed to show up, thus: "I am disgusted with myself and the whole Negro set, God dam' em!"[2]

As the only Black survivor of the seizure of Harper's Ferry, as one who escaped the slave-holder's hanging for armed revolt, and as one who bore arms in defense of freedom and in furtherance of the establishment of a free Black republic in the mountains of the Appalachians, Anderson was in a perfect position to speak to the issue of slave betrayal. Instead, he sees none. He found the slaves supportive and overjoyed by the revolt, and counts them among the first to fall from the armed conflict. He was among the contingent that visited the plantations, where he found "the greatest enthusiasm":

[J]oy and hilarity beamed from every countenance. One old mother, white-haired from age, and borne down with the labors of many years in bonds, when told of the work in hand, replied: "God bless you! God bless you!"

Anderson found volunteers, who stepped forward "manfully" to assist the cause. Indeed, the only hesitation he found was among so-called "free" Blacks: "A dark-complexioned free-born man refused to take up arms. He showed the only want of confidence in the movement, and far less courage than any slave consulted about the plan."

The truth of the Harper's Ferry "raid," as it has been called, in regard to the part taken by the slaves, and the aid given by colored men generally, demonstrates clearly: First, that the conduct of the slaves is a strong guarantee of the weakness of the institution, should a favorable opportunity occur; and, secondly, that the colored people, as a body, were well represented by numbers, both in the fight, and in the number who suffered martyrdom afterward.

Of the seventeen revolutionaries who died at Harper's Ferry, *nine were Black men!* Moreover, five Black men were among the twenty-three revolutionaries who waged the action, and only one (Anderson) successfully escaped the battle. This means that the majority of men who died at the Ferry were Black men; *the majority of Black men who fought and died* (five of nine) *were slaves fighting for their freedom!*

---

[2] Ibid., 205.

Have you ever read such a thing in your history books? Have you ever even got that impression from any previous rendition of the assault of John Brown's troops on Harper's Ferry?

There is an old saying: "History is written by the victor." Thus, much of what we claim to know is that which was preserved and projected by the slave-holders, who prevailed at Harper's Ferry, aided as they were by the Virginia and Maryland militias, as well as a company of U.S. Marines. History is also a work of suppression, and a silencing of views that challenge the prevailing narrative.

Osborne Anderson's *A Voice from Harper's Ferry* shatters that silence, and speaks with a calm and moving intelligence that shows the reasons the attack was launched, the intensity of feelings which preceded it, and the genuine respect that Brown engendered in his troops. That these twenty-three men could work together, fight together, and some die together in pursuit of liberty is a powerful testimony that continues to resonate in us almost a century and a half later. What you have here is hidden history, written by one who actually lived a life in resistance to a great evil—human slavery.

American poet Henry Wadsworth Longfellow wrote in his diary for 2 December 1859 (the date of Brown's execution), "This will be a great day in our history, the date of a new Revolution—quite as much needed as the old one."[3] Some sixteen months later, Southern rebels would fire on Fort Sumter, a federal installation located in the self-described Republic of South Carolina, the first state to secede from the Union, and a state of Civil War would be pronounced. When Union soldiers marched into Dixie, many of them were singing "John Brown's Body." In a sense, they were but reinforcements, who took two years to heed his call, to deliver a death blow to the hated system of human bondage, sounded loudly on 17 October 1859.

25 June 1999

Death Row / Waynesburg, Pa.

---

[3] Ibid., 210.

What is a nation?

By Monica Moorehead

What is the definition of a nation? People seem to take for granted that the U.S., France, and Britain, for example, are nations. Are not most of us indoctrinated from day one with the idea that the U.S. is "one nation under God with liberty and justice for all"? But this view ignores the fact that there are millions of people living within these countries who suffer consistent oppression, not just because of their class—what they do for a living and what they own—but simply because of who they are.

Some might say a nation is a group of people who share a common language, common heritage, and common borders. But this gives only a partial answer. V.I. Lenin, writing from the experience of building a revolutionary multi-national workers' party in czarist Russia, taught that there are nations within nations. There are nations that oppress and nations that are oppressed.

Take France, for instance. France has historically colonized and plundered whole areas of Africa, oppressing African nations. However, within France today there are also vast communities of oppressed people who were forced to migrate from those former colonies to seek a better life—people from Mali, Algeria, Ivory Coast, and Vietnam, for example. Their status of being members of an oppressed nation does not change just because they have moved geographically to inside the oppressor nation.

The question of national oppression is not just about Third World nations and not just about skin color. National oppression grows out of the expansion of capitalism worldwide and its built-in drive for super-exploitation. Therefore, the struggle against national oppression hits at the heart of imperialism.

The Irish have been nationally oppressed by the English ruling class for over 800 years. The Basque people have been trying to win political recognition of their national identity from Spain, and many have supported an armed struggle against the oppressor. Imperialist Japan in 1910 annexed all Korea as its colony. Before World War II it seized part of China, and set up colonial administrations in much of the rest of Asia that supplanted European colonizers—Britain, France, Holland, and Portugal—as well as the United States.

The United States even today has outright colonies in Puerto Rico, Guam, and the Virgin Islands—in addition to its domination over scores of other countries through economic control and military pressure. These nations are oppressed in relation to imperialism. But what about inside the U.S.?

In the U.S., the billionaire ruling class that controls all the industries, agribusiness, and the banks is almost exclusively white. In addition to being an exploiting capitalist class, it also heads up an oppressor nation. Within the borders of the U.S. are many different oppressed peoples, including African Americans, Native nations, Puerto Ricans, Mexicans/Chicanos, Palestinians, Jamaicans, Haitians, Arabs, Dominicans, and many others.

All these oppressed nations have had their own unique social and historical evolution. But one thing they all have in common is being super-exploited and super-oppressed by imperialism. Although all whites in the U.S. belong to the oppressor nation, there is a big difference between the white bourgeoisie and the white working class.

The labor of the white workers is exploited by the capitalists—although, on a whole, not as intensively as that of the nationally oppressed workers. However, as capitalist restructuring and megamergers proceed, with mass layoffs and union busting, more and more whites find themselves sharing, even though to a somewhat lesser degree, the fate that for some decades seemed relegated to the oppressed people—low wages, loss of benefits, and so on.

In his theses for the Second Congress of the Communist International written back in 1920, Lenin, the leader of the 1917 Russian Revolution, mentioned the special oppression of Black or African

Americans in the U.S. as very significant for the worldwide proletarian movement at the time. It still is today.

Marxists argue that no economic, political, or social phenomenon can be fully understood without taking into account its historical development. No struggle takes place within a vacuum; no struggle is isolated from the general laws of nature and society. Marxists are materialists, not idealists. Marxists know that being determines consciousness—that what people think does not drop from the sky but is conditioned by their social experiences.

To fully understand the Black struggle or the Black experience in the U.S. and its status today, we have to view its development in relationship to the overall class struggle. The Black struggle in this country has many rich lessons for us as workers, as progressives, and as revolutionaries. Exploring the Black revolution in relationship to the class struggle will help to understand why only socialism can liberate all of humanity from this nightmare known as capitalism.

Every struggle for national liberation is crucial to building class solidarity. Any characterization that pits oppressed groups against each other or makes us compete over the question of who's more persecuted or oppressed is harmful. Oppression in any form is degrading, dehumanizing, and unnatural.

Karl Marx wrote that the dominant ideas of any time are defined by the ideas of the ruling class. None of the working-class or oppressed communities is immune ideologically from the daily doses of ABC, NBC, or CBS. For instance, every year McDonald's, Burger King, and other big corporations like to define for us what Black History Month should mean—they want us to see it from their own bourgeois, narrow view.

Black history, however, is not just about who invented what. It's not just about all the wonderful African American artists, athletes, historians, and educators who were able to rise above racism and prejudice in their own way to make contributions to the betterment of all society in the areas of science, popular culture, and the arts.

What is most important 365 days a year is that since the time the first African slave set foot on this soil, the African American struggle for national liberation has been part of the overall class struggle to liberate humanity.

This is what none of the history books will teach us—that the Black struggle today is part and parcel of the struggle for socialism, that is, the struggle to reconstruct human society and abolish all classes. Further, our struggle is not just about emphasizing great individuals, but about social and political movements and class upheavals.

While the history books given our children in school devote some space to a dynamic person like Dr. Martin Luther King, Jr., they spend little time on the mass movement he led and what conditions gave rise to it. It was the strength and momentum of this movement that won progressive gains like civil rights legislation for the Southern Black masses, even if only within the framework of bourgeois legality.

But to understand why the civil rights movement had to take place, to understand the Black Panthers or even the controversy surrounding the Nation of Islam, we have to go back some 100 years to a period known as Reconstruction. What was Reconstruction? It was the post-Civil War period that began in 1866 and abruptly and tragically ended in 1877. It marked the rebuilding of the South and the process of enfranchising an estimated 4 million Black former slaves, who had been stripped of all political and economic freedoms under cruel, inhuman bondage.

During Reconstruction the U.S. government set up Freedmen's Bureau agencies throughout the South. Their stated goal was to oversee the establishment of institutions that would help provide literacy, land, and total suffrage for the freed people, all under the protection of federal troops. That this purpose was betrayed does not negate the fact that Reconstruction was an important attempt to win full economic and political rights for Black people under the early stages of capitalist development in the U.S.

Osborne Anderson's stirring eyewitness account, *A Voice from Harper's Ferry*, helped to explain an important episode in the struggle to destroy slavery and lay the basis for Reconstruction.

Many books with diverse interpretations have been written on the Reconstruction period. Three exceptional ones were used for this brief overview. The first, by the great Marxist scholar W.E.B. Du Bois, is called *Black Reconstruction in America.* The second is by another Marxist, James S. Allen, and is called *Reconstruction: The Battle for Democracy, 1875-1876.* And the third, called *Background for Radical Reconstruction,* contains many important documents and was edited by Hans L. Trefousse.

The Civil War between the North and the South, which resulted in at least half a million people losing their lives, was not fought to bring an end to chattel slavery for some 4 million people of African descent. It was not a war between oppressed and oppressor.

It was a class war between two different exploiting classes; it was a war between two social systems.

On one side was the outmoded slavocracy, which was even more oppressive than the feudal landlord class overthrown in Europe in the 1848 bourgeois revolutions.

On the other side was the budding capitalist class in the North that needed industrialization, the expansion of the railroads, and pioneer settlements throughout the West. The West was still inhabited by the Native nations, but they were being systemically driven off the best land and exterminated by the genocidal methods of the U.S. government and cavalry. The U.S. had just taken over at least one half of Mexico in the war of 1846 to 1848.

The slaves in the South faced conditions very similar to those of the serfs in feudal Europe. The slaves were like the serfs and the slave masters like the lords. The difference was that the slave had no rights and was owned outright by the slave owner, whose brutality was tempered only by his financial interest in preserving his "property." Du Bois eloquently speaks on this in his book:

Slaves were not considered men. They had no right of petition. They were 'devisable like any other chattel.' They could own nothing; they could make no contracts; they could hold no property, nor traffic in property; they could not hire out; they could not legally marry nor constitute families; they could not control their children.... They could not testify in court.... A slave [had] no right to education or religion.... A slave might be condemned to death for striking any white person.[4]

The slaves had no control over any aspect of their lives, including no right to sell their ability to work in exchange for wages.

And what was the relationship of the white workers in the North and South to the slaves? In the North, industrial capitalism was on the rise and a trade union movement was in formation. Many of these workers were first-generation immigrants escaping poverty and oppression in Europe.

Some white workers were very sympathetic to the plight of the slaves; many became active in the abolitionist movement. But even in the North, there was much racism toward the slaves and the free Black people who had managed either to buy their freedom or escape from slavery.

Many white workers in lower-paid, menial jobs viewed Black people as competitors and accused them of driving down wages. Unfortunately, most leaders of the craft unions then in existence did not instill within the workers a class view that the Northern industrialists and the slavocracy were both their enemies and that their fight should be not only for the abolition of slavery but for the full equality of Black people.

These white workers were ignorant of the reality that it's the bosses who drive down wages, not oppressed Black labor. During the 1830s, before the Civil War, a number of race riots took place. In Cincinnati and Philadelphia, Black people were killed by racist mobs. Many freed slaves emigrated to Canada to escape this repression.

On the other hand, some white workers who had come from England and Germany were more class-conscious on the question of fighting the slavocracy and understood the need for class solidarity with the slaves. Many of these workers had been influenced by the 1848 revolutions and brought those experiences to the U.S. In fact, the First International Workingmen's Association, based in England

---

[4] W.E.B. Du Bois, *Black Reconstruction in America* (New York: S.A. Russell Co., 1956), 10.

and founded by Karl Marx and others, came out militantly against chattel and wage slavery.

It was Marx who made the famous statement, "Labor cannot emancipate itself in the white skin where in the black it is branded."[5] In other words, the struggle against capitalism as a system of wage slavery is inseparably linked to the political and economic emancipation of Black people.

In the South, there were an estimated 5 million white workers and farmers, the majority of them very poor and without slaves. These whites were for the most part also without land because the big landowners or planters controlled most of it. Some poor whites called for the overthrow of the landlords, but did not call for an alliance with the slaves. As a general rule most landless Southern whites would have opted to become brutal overseers in hope of one day rising to the status of a planter.

The slaves had no really formidable allies within the South. They had no choice but to look to the North—where some whites were sympathetic—as the only option to freedom. With the outbreak of the Civil War, thousands of slaves took the opportunity to escape, not giving it even a second thought that they were "violating" the Fugitive Slave Act of 1850. This act stated that any escaped slave could be legally caught outside the boundaries of the slave states and brought back to the plantations. The Dred Scott decision by the Supreme Court in 1857 reaffirmed slavery in the new territories of the West.

Dred Scott

This brings up a point not often raised about the Civil War and the role of President Abraham Lincoln. As it became more and more possible that a war would erupt around the question of the expansion of slavery vs. its containment, Lincoln did not behave as the great friend or emancipator of the slaves he has been made out to be. He was more concerned about whether slavery

---

[5] Karl Marx, *Capital* (New York: International Publishers, 1977), vol. 1, 301.

would spread to Kansas or Colorado or some other area in the West on which the capitalists had set their sights for expansion. In fact, there was real concern in the North and South that a guerrilla movement made up of abolitionists and ex-slaves, like the one led by John Brown, might try to free every slave in the country.

Lincoln actually endorsed the return of "fugitive" slaves to their masters early in the war. It was only after many slaves had escaped their inhumane situation that Lincoln was forced to sign into law the Emancipation Proclamation of 1863, which ratified what had already taken place.

You could say that at least 500,000 slaves were carrying out their version of a general strike against intolerable conditions. A similar situation occurred in 1965, when President Lyndon Johnson was forced to sign civil rights legislation because the masses were demonstrating in the hundreds of thousands for it.

Were it not for escaping slaves joining the Union Army in the tens of thousands, the North could have lost the war militarily. Before Black men were given guns, they performed such tasks as cooks, spies, and personal assistants to the Union officers.

At first, the Union Army discouraged Black men from joining its ranks; some officers even attempted to deport these ex-slaves back to the South. But so many white troops deserted that the Union Army had no choice but to accept Black men, especially after they had "proved" themselves on the battlefield. The Confederate legislature even considered passing a bill to allow the recruitment of slaves into its army in order to stop the flow of the slaveholders' "property" to the Union Army. But the slavocracy was forced to surrender before the law was enacted.

What is crucial to understand about the surrender of the Confederacy is that it was primarily of a military character. The U.S. government under the tutelage of the Northern bourgeoisie took some measures to confiscate the lands of the former slave owners and put them under the jurisdiction of the federal government. But they did not smash the slavocracy as a class. They refused to uproot every vestige of slavery.

This served to deter a transition from a reactionary feudal period to a bourgeois democracy in the South, at least as far as the Black masses were concerned.

This abandonment of the freed slaves on the part of the Northern bourgeoisie laid the basis for the racist, terrorist counter-revolution that was to take place, which gave birth to the Ku Klux Klan, White Citizens Councils, and others.

The freed people did have some allies in the Congress in the form of the Radical Republicans, led by Thaddeus Stevens and Charles Sumner. The Radical Republicans were the left wing of the Republican Party. Both men were strong advocates for bourgeois democracy, but Stevens was the more radical of the two. He initiated strong legislation that could have brought political equality for the ex-slaves and economic empowerment as well—especially where the question of land was concerned.

Once again, this type of progressive legislation was confirming legally what was already taking place. Even before the Emancipation Proclamation was signed, Black people took it upon themselves to confiscate the land that they had made productive and divided it up among themselves.

This began to occur wherever the Northern troops armed the slaves after overrunning Confederate positions. On the other hand, there were times when the Union Army would intervene and put down slave insurrections. In the "Ogeechee Negro rebellion," some five to twelve hundred armed slaves tried to take over the plantations near Savannah, Georgia.

The main issue during the post-Civil War Reconstruction period was the seizure of the land in the South. The most famous of these battles for land took place in the Sea Islands off the coast of Charleston, South Carolina. This was a valiant struggle, indeed, when you consider that by this time the White House was occupied by a sympathizer with the slavocracy—Andrew Johnson—who had become president following the assassination of Lincoln.

On May 29, 1865, Johnson issued a proclamation giving unconditional amnesty to those who fought on the side of the Confederacy.

All they had to do was take an oath of loyalty to the U.S. government. High-ranking Confederate officers and those planters who controlled more than $20,000 (a very large sum in 1865) were given a slap on the wrist for their crimes against humanity.

Johnson appointed provisional governors within the Southern states who allowed the amnestied voters to resume seats in their respective state governments. Instead of ordering the federal troops to root out and destroy every vestige of the slavocracy, Johnson's traitorous actions allowed the former Confederate ruling circles back into the driver's seat.

The ex-plantations in the Sea Islands were occupied by Black people a year after the Civil War ended. When the U.S. government made attempts to legally restore these islands to the former slave masters, armed guerrilla fighters organized some successful resistance to secure their settlements. These freedmen were exercising their right to seize lands that their slave labor had made productive but which had enriched the privileged slavocracy.

In 1866 and 1867, Congress held hearings of the Joint Committee on Reconstruction. Many witnesses from the North and South, Black and white, testified on the economic, political, and military conditions following the Civil War.

Brigadier General Charles H. Howard was brother of the head of the Freedmen's Bureau and an inspector for the bureau in Charleston, South Carolina. In his testimony, Howard testified on the conditions of the newly freed Black masses in the Sea Islands.

Question: Can you state how these islands are now principally occupied?

Howard: A number of plantations on each, and sometime entire islands, have been formally restored to their former owners. They were all abandoned during the war. On several of the islands Negroes have been located and have been engaged in cultivating the land. Some, and a considerable number, previously to General Sherman's celebrated order [setting aside a strip along the coast for the use of black farmers], issued last winter at Savannah, and a large number under the provisions of that order, have been located on the different islands. A considerable number have received formal titles to forty acres each on these islands. Where there were large numbers of them on any given plantation they still remain in possession; but where there were very few on a plantation, the plantation has been, in some cases, restored. The understanding was that the orders were that where there were very few Negroes on a plantation the plantation should be restored if the Negroes were properly provided with homes.[6]

General Rufus Saxton, a military governor of the Sea Islands, became assistant commissioner of the Freedmen's Bureau. He was removed from his position by President Andrew Johnson for refusing to carry out orders requiring him to restore Black people's lands in the Sea Islands to the Confederacy. Here is part of his testimony:

> *Question:* Are you aware that the blacks have arms to any considerable extent in South Carolina?
> *Saxton:* I believe that a great many of them have arms, and I know it to be their earnest desire to procure them.... I can further state that [former Confederate soldiers called Regulators] desired me to sanction a form of contract which would deprive the colored men of their arms, which I refused to do. The subject was so important, as I thought, to the welfare of the freedmen that I issued a circular on this subject, which circular not having been approved by the military commander was not published, as I was required by my instructions to get his approval to all my circulars before I issued them.... I will further add, that I believe it to be the settled purpose of the white people of South Carolina to be armed and thoroughly organized, and to have the whole black population thoroughly disarmed and defenseless; I believe that is the settled policy.
> *Question:* What would be the probable effect of such an effort to disarm the blacks?
> *Saxton:* It would subject them to the severest oppression, and leave their condition no better than before they were emancipated, and in many respects worse than it was before.[7]

A number of Black conventions were organized throughout the South for the purpose of organizing mass opposition to the Johnson government and the reactionary Black Codes—as well as to help the ex-slaves continue upon their revolutionary path for complete democracy. What were the Black Codes? These codes were passed by the ex-plantation owners and were really no different from the slave codes. While each Southern state was allowed to enact its own codes, they were generally the same.

Here is how historian James Allen described them:

---

[6] *Background for Radical Reconstruction,* edited by Hans L. Trefousse (Boston: Little, Brown and Company, 1970), 45.

[7] Ibid., 39.

The Black Codes can be compared with the vagrancy acts of Western Europe at the end of the 15th and through the 16th centuries. Due to the breaking up of the feudal estates of Western Europe, a large body of future proletarians were cut loose from the land and from their masters. Industry, however, could not yet absorb them and the vagrancy laws were used to imprison and put to forced labor this large landless and jobless mass. In the South, 4,000,000 Negro slaves had become masterless. There was no industry to absorb them; they were propelled instead towards seizing large landed estates. Counter-revolution replied with the Black Codes, consisting of vagrancy and apprenticeship acts designed to force Negroes to labor on the plantations under conditions imposed by the planters.[8]

The Freedmen's Bureau, established by the federal government under President Grant to help establish schools and social services for ex-slaves, stated in a report that the Black Codes "actually served to secure to the former slave-holding class the unpaid labor which they had been accustomed to enjoy before the war."[9]

A number of freed Black people were asked to provide testimony on the issue of wages under Reconstruction. Oscar J. Dunn was a runaway slave who bought his freedom and eventually resided in New Orleans. He was elected lieutenant governor of Louisiana and served from 1868 until 1871.

Question: Has there been a branch of the Freedmen's Bureau here in the city?

Dunn: Yes, sir; and I have had occasion to send a great many freedmen to it. The planters, in many portions of the state, would make arrangements with them and fail to perform their part of the contract. There have been many instances the present season where planters have employed laborers at $15 a month. The contract specified that the planter should be allowed to retain one-half the monthly salary; they would retain it in that way until the cotton was picked, and then manage to get into a quarrel with them and drive them away without paying them. I have had several come to me with such information, and some of them I have taken to the Freedmen's Bureau. This is a common thing through all the parishes. The Freedmen's Bureau is a great eyesore to the planters; they do not like it all; and I am sorry to say that in many instances agents in the parishes do not act exactly just towards the freedmen.[10]

---

[8] James S. Allen, Reconstruction: The Battle for Democracy (New York: International Publishers, 1937), 58.

[9] Ibid., 59.

[10] *Background*, 4.

Daniel Norton was a Black physician who practiced medicine during the Civil War in Virginia.

Question: How do the returned rebels treat the colored people?

Norton: They have in some cases treated them well, but in more cases they have not. A number of persons living in the country have come into Yorktown and reported to the Freedmen's Bureau that they have not been treated well; that they worked all the year and had received no pay, and were driven off on the first of January. They say that the owners with whom they had been living rented out their places, sold their crops, and told them they had no further use for them, and that they might go to the Yankees....

The slaveholders, who have owned them, say that they will take them back, but cannot pay them any wages. Some are willing to pay a dollar a month, and some less, and some are only willing to give them their clothing and what they eat. They are not willing to pay anything for work....

Question: In case of the removal of the military force from among you, and also of the Freedmen's Bureau, what would the whites do with you?

Norton: I do not think that the colored people would be safe. They would be in danger of being hunted and killed. The spirit of the whites against the blacks is much worse than it was before the war; a white gentleman with whom I was talking made this remark: he said he was well disposed toward the colored people, but that finding that they took up arms against him, he had come to the conclusion that he never wanted to have anything to do with them, or to show any spirit of kindness toward them. These were his sentiments.[11]

The Black people did what they could to turn back this growing counter-revolution. Besides arming themselves in self-defense, they participated in Constitutional Conventions throughout the South where, for the first time, Black people voted for their own representatives. In many instances, the Black representatives were still outnumbered by whites.

But in the South Carolina Reconstruction legislature, 84 of the 157 representatives were Black. In fact, South Carolina and Louisiana had the two predominantly Black parliaments in the South. These delegates represented the left wing of the parliaments. They initiated laws that would benefit both Black and poor white people in opposition to the ex-plantation owners.

---

[11] Ibid., 11-12.

It is important to return to the question of the role of the labor movement during the Reconstruction era. As we said, class-conscious German immigrants played an active role in fighting slavery. Many joined the Union Army; others joined the Radical Republicans; still others formed Communist Clubs.

Among the German emigrés who migrated to the South to fight against the slavocracy were Hermann Meyer, a member of the International Working Men's Association, and Adolph Douai. Meyer and Douai were both forced to leave the South because of their bold activities. The trade union movement as a whole, however, while demanding an end to slavery, did not make any real attempts to integrate Black workers into the then predominantly white male workers' movement.

The trade union leaders in the North saw the Black workers as unskilled competitors with white labor. This attitude made it easier for the Northern capitalists to bring in Black scab workers when a strike occurred, in order to further divide Black against white. The same tactic was used against low-paid Chinese laborers, who provided the backbone for building the railroads in the West.

The biggest strategic mistake that the northern trade union movement made was not to recognize and unconditionally support the political and economic struggle of the newly emerged Black workers. Black workers were therefore forced to organize their own trade union organizations—laying the basis for segregated shops. This did not stop these Black workers from taking internationalist and class-conscious positions on a number of questions.

For instance, at the Colored National Labor Convention in Washington, D.C., in 1869, resolutions were passed in support of Black and women's suffrage, along with one supporting the Cuban struggle against Spanish colonialism. Their platform also called for equality in industry and protested discriminatory practices within trade unions. Free immigration for all nationalities was accepted. At the same time, Chinese labor—known then as "coolie" labor, a racist term—was labeled "slavery in a new form."

This is not to say that there were no links between Black trade union leaders and the trade union movement. The International Workingmen's Association in Chicago carried out political activities in the Black community there. In 1872 a split-off section of the IWA nominated the great Frederick Douglass and Victoria Woodhull, a leader in the women's suffrage movement, for vice-president and president of the United States, respectively.

On September 13, 1871, at a march calling for the eight-hour day, members of the Black waiters' union and Black plasterers' union marched in the IWA contingent. These Black workers received some of the biggest applause from the onlookers, who were chanting "Vive la Commune" in response to the Paris Commune uprising.

And just three months later, on December 18, 1871, a Black militia known as the Skidmore Guard participated in a demonstration to protest the execution of three leading Parisian Communards. So despite any racial barriers, Black workers contributed greatly to the advancement of the U.S. labor movement and also the growing socialist movement.

As Black people continued to make political gains in the South, the ex-slave owners and their allies tried every maneuver to advance the counter-revolution. When the divide-and-conquer tactic of splitting the Black masses from the Radical Republicans failed, alongside attempts to attract Black people to the conservative Democrat Party, these racists looked toward the backward white masses for the answer—through a campaign of whipping up hysteria based on white supremacy. Tragically, the majority of the white masses eventually succumbed to this most dangerous of all divide-and-conquer schemes.

Clandestine racist terrorist organizations sprang up throughout the South to attack organized meetings of Black representatives and progressive anti-racist whites.

The KKK had been around since 1865, when it was founded in Pulaski, Tennessee, by a group of ex-Confederate officers. The former slave masters regained authority in North Carolina when the federal government refused to send troops to crush Klan-organized terror. In fact, the final blow came when the Union Army was withdrawn from the South in the period 1876 to 1877. This marked the decisive betrayal of the Reconstruction era, ushering in a new stage of outright fascistic reaction.

The Black people were forced into a situation of semi-slavery. They and the revolutionary institutions they had fought so hard for were now left defenseless by those they had thought were their Northern allies. In the meantime, the KKK was on its way to becoming an instrument of state terror on behalf of the capitalist repressive state.

In his book, *The Klan and the Government—Foes or Allies?*, Sam Marcy, chair of Workers World Party, wrote that

...the KKK is not merely an organization that grew up autonomously and spontaneously to promote racism. It is an offspring of the capitalist state of which the Southern states once again became an integral part. The Klan has always been part and parcel, sometimes secretly, sometimes openly, of the capitalist state, especially in the police and military forces of the U.S. ... Their targets vary from time to time, but their general objective is the same—the destruction of the democratic rights of the workers and oppressed. They are the closest approximation to a fascist apparatus. Always they grow out of a period of acute class struggle.[12]

The period following Reconstruction led to the outbreak of lynchings throughout the South. Over 3,000 lynchings were officially recorded from the late 1800s through the 1920s. This prompted Vietnamese leader Ho Chi Minh to characterize African Americans as "one of the most oppressed groupings of people on earth."

In the historic *Plessy vs. Ferguson* ruling in 1898, the U.S. Supreme Court institutionalized segregation throughout the South and many areas of the North with the infamous "Jim Crow" laws.

So how did the defeat of Reconstruction impact on the Black struggle and the class struggle in general against capitalism in this country? What is the common thread running through every one of these struggles? What various forms have these struggles taken?

---

[12] Sam Marcy, *The Klan and the Government—Foes or Allies?* (New York, World View Publishers, 1983), 36-37.

These periods hold very rich lessons for the working class and all the oppressed. This brief essay cannot do justice to them.

One important figure was Booker T. Washington, a Black educator. Notwithstanding his political conservatism and accommodation to the capitalist establishment, Washington founded Tuskegee Institute (now University), in Tuskegee, Alabama, several years after the collapse of Reconstruction. Washington appealed to Northern industrialists to help finance the first of many important agricultural and industrial colleges in the southern Black Belt to encourage former slaves and their descendants to become self-reliant and independent from their former slave masters.

There was the founding of the National Association for the Advancement of Colored People by W.E.B. Du Bois and other members of the Niagara Movement. Their aim was to organize mass and legal opposition to the lynchings, including legal lynchings of Black men by the racist courts.

There was the mass movement known as the Universal Negro Improvement Association, led by Marcus Garvey in the early 1900s, which advocated Black people going back to Africa. Whether one agreed with the program or not, this anti-colonial movement galvanized more than a million Black people in the struggle.

And then there was the civil rights movement that propelled millions of people, Black and white, to pick up the torch left by the freed people following slavery and Reconstruction to fight the Jim Crow laws. The civil rights struggle was also a forerunner to the gay and women's liberation movements.

There was the Black Panther Party inspired by the great Malcolm X and founded by Huey P. Newton and Bobby Seale in 1967. This was the most revolutionary party within the Black community until it was decimated by the FBI and the U.S. government in the early 1970s. This organization called for the armed self-defense of Black and other oppressed peoples against the repressive state—the cops, the courts, the FBI, and so on.

They considered themselves internationalists in solidarity with revolutionary struggles in Africa, Asia, Latin America, and the Middle East as well as other struggles in this country. In fact, Panther leader Huey Newton wrote a document in the early 1970s in support of the gay struggle, calling upon progressives to ally themselves with the gay movement.

Capitalist democracy in the U.S. has proven incapable of solving racism and the national question as well as other forms of oppression—let alone economic inequality. After all, it has been over a century since Reconstruction, yet deep inequality remains.

Bourgeois democracy is but a form of capitalist rule. After all is said and done, capitalist democracy serves the rich and the super-rich. The explosion of the prison-industrial complex exposes the utter bankruptcy of bourgeois democracy and the deepening repression that it heaps upon the poor, especially people of color. The statistics speak for themselves.

The U.S. has the largest prison population in the world—1.8 million people. This number is expected to rise to 2 million by the year 2000. It equals the combined populations of Atlanta, St. Louis, Pittsburgh, Des Moines, and Miami. The California state system is actually the biggest in the Western industrialized world—and is 40 percent larger than the Federal Bureau of Prisons. California alone has more people incarcerated in its jails and prisons than the prison populations of France, Great Britain, Germany, Japan, Singapore, and the Netherlands put together.

Since 1991, the rate of violent acts has decreased by 20 percent while the number of people in prison has increased by 50 percent.

Due to a decline in drug rehabilitation programs on the outside and an increase in drug-related arrests and harsh convictions with racial disparities, close to one half of the prisoners in the U.S. are African American. One out of fourteen Black men is incarcerated. One out of every four Black men is likely to be caught up in the vicious web of the criminal justice system at some point during his lifetime.

The number of women prisoners—now 80,000—has multiplied by twelve since 1970. Many are locked up for alleged drug-related offenses and other nonviolent acts. Seventy-five percent of these women are mothers; African Americans make up the largest group.

Seventy percent of the prisoners in the U.S. are illiterate. An estimated 200,000 have a serious mental illness. While 60 percent to 80 percent have a substance addiction, only one out of every ten inmates receives any kind of drug treatment in prison.

What are the economic factors regarding prisons? Private corporations are investing an estimated $35 billion annually in some aspect of the prison-industrial complex. This includes some of the largest architectural and construction firms, along with Wall Street investment banks that pour millions of dollars into supporting prison bond issues and the privatization of prisons. The telephone conglomerates are raking in profits by the fistful off of prisons.

The expansion of prisons has had a big impact in impoverished rural areas. With devastating layoffs in other industries, prison construction has created an economic boom in correctional jobs and has led to the growth of other related industries. This is especially true of New York State—two thirds of the state's counties are classified as rural. One county that had only two prisons a quarter of a century ago today has eighteen and a nineteenth under construction. The town of Dannemora has more inmates than free people.

A captive work force can make super-profits for local, state, and national governments—and slave labor can be pitted against other workers with better paying jobs.

Prisoners are often forced into taking jobs that unionized workers could be doing—like telemarketing for big commercial firms. Shouldn't the unions make it their business to organize these prisoners, and demand union wages and conditions, so they can't be used as scab labor?

Even as prisons are privatized, the U.S. government is spending more money on jails than ever before. In 1996 Washington spent more money on prison construction than on university construction—almost a billion dollars. This was the same year that President Bill Clinton signed away welfare. The Clinton administration has also outdone its Republican predecessors in placing "illegal aliens" and minimum-security inmates into private prisons.

The bottom line is this: under capitalism, investors and bankers will put their money into any sector of the economy, no matter how anti-human it may be, in order to maximize profits. This is not a matter of policy but is based on the independent laws of capitalist development that drive big business to gravitate to wherever the rate of profit is highest.

There are more than three thousand political prisoners in the U.S. These heroic women and men, the majority of them from nationally oppressed communities, either entered prison as activists during the 1960s and 1970s or became political in jail—like the murdered Panther leader, George Jackson. They all have at least two things in common: they stand against racist repression and other forms of injustice, and the capitalist state wants to silence them. The 1971 Attica prison rebellion for a brief moment exposed the hideous oppression behind the walls and the existence of political prisoners.

Many political prisoners are well known, like Leonard Peltier, the MOVE 9 and the remaining Puerto Rican political prisoners.

The most recognized prisoner on death row is Mumia Abu-Jamal, "the voice of the voiceless." Mumia is more than just another innocent man, like so many who languish in apartheid-like dungeons. In the eyes of the U.S. government, he is "guilty" of being an uncompromising, unwavering revolutionary who has helped to expose police brutality, the death penalty, and other forms of racist atrocities since he became a member of the Black Panther Party as a teenager.

Mumia's fight for a new trial has stimulated unity among progressives and revolutionaries of all nationalities and ages. The struggle to free Mumia and all political prisoners is tied to the overall struggle against a class system that persecutes the poor, workers, the oppressed, and all who resist the tiny clique of parasitic bosses and bankers.

Any discussion of the evils of capitalism leads inevitably to the next question: what can replace it? Only the socialist revolution, a revolution achieved through the organization of the working class and all the oppressed. That is what all the struggles of modern times have come down to: the need to reorganize society to serve human needs and not to pile up profits for a small class on top.

Only socialist revolution can fully emancipate all people of color, along with the entire working class on a worldwide scale. The collapse of the Soviet Union and the bloc of countries allied to it may have been a terrible blow, but the class struggle will be revitalized there and throughout the world. The horrible conditions for the workers and the revival of vicious national antagonisms that have accompanied the restoration of capitalism there prove once again—even if by negative example—that only socialism can establish true democracy based on the workers of all nationalities running society in a cooperative manner.

William Mandel, the author of *Soviet But Not Russian*, a book about the great progress made by the many nationalities during the time of the Soviet Union, talks about what socialism might look like in the U.S.: "Imagine that Third World people in the U.S. were employed in the mass media in proportion to their number in the population, one in five—eight times their present representation, which is one in forty. Imagine a Black governor of Mississippi, statues of Dr. W.E.B. Du Bois, Paul Robeson, Harriet Tubman, Martin Luther King, and Malcolm X on the State House lawn in Richmond, Virginia, instead of the generals who fought for slavery, which stand there now. Imagine the children of Spanish-speaking farmworkers not being taken out of school to follow the crops. Imagine an Eskimo woman as governor of Alaska, like the Chukchi woman who governs the Soviet territory that faces Alaska across the Bering Straits."[13]

Sam Marcy really said it best:

A working class party such as Lenin tried to build should promote every right that a Black person is deprived of that a white one has achieved. We promote and must propagate the right to self-determination, but which road to take for liberation must be decided by the oppressed nation itself.

A revolutionary working-class party promotes class solidarity irrespective of which option an oppressed nation chooses. The neutrality of the party in this respect is the strongest pillar of working-class multinational solidarity in the struggle against capitalism and imperialism.

---

[13] William M. Mandel, *Soviet but not Russian* (Edmonton, Canada: University of Alberta Press, 1985), 34.

The bourgeoisie denies and closes the road to both separatism and integration. They neither wish to complete the bourgeois democratic revolution for political equality nor allow social and economic equality. Nor will they permit the development of a movement for an independent separate state....

[T]he whole struggle of the working class as well as the oppressed people and their allies everywhere is to recognize that there can be no real independence, freedom, or equality as long as the monstrous system of capitalist exploitation and imperialist oppression remains. The struggle for any and all concessions must and will go on, and each concession won is a building block in the struggle for emancipation from imperialist finance capital.[14]

---

[14] Sam Marcy, "Black nationalism and white chauvinism: Marxism and national oppression," *Workers World*, May 17, 1984.

The unfinished revolution

**By Vince
Copeland**

Much has been written about the Harper's Ferry raid. But Osborne P. Anderson's story—in the words of W.E.B. Du Bois "the most interesting and reliable account of the raid"—has a special significance that has been too long neglected.

First, Anderson was one of the actual participants, and being Black, he might be expected to have a somewhat different view of the affair than even the most inspired white supporter of John Brown. Second, he apparently wrote the pamphlet with the hope of encouraging a general slave insurrection. And third, he obviously expected other whites to imitate the action of John Brown and help supply the arms for the insurrection, as well as take up arms themselves.

He was interested, like most other Black and white abolitionists of that very revolutionary period, in continuing the revolution that John Brown's band had begun. But he seems to have based his optimism upon the possibilities of slave insurrection, rather more than upon white support, which he must have thought of as an important auxiliary force rather than as the main body of struggle.

He took pains to emphasize the number of slaves who accepted guns the moment guns were offered to them. He pointed out what few subsequent narrators of the event have: namely that *of the seventeen revolutionaries who died at Harper's Ferry* (before the legal lynching of Brown and the others after the trial), *nine were Black.*

Eight whites and two Blacks of the original band were killed in the conflict in addition to the hastily armed seven Black slaves. Two other Blacks were executed with Brown.

History has finally given Brown tremendous credit for what was indeed a tremendous feat. But Brown had been planning it for decades and the others in the band had been thinking for months and for years about how to strike this dramatic blow. What about the seven nameless Black people who died for Black freedom with no prior notice whatever?

They, too, no doubt, had thought for years about freedom—their own freedom. They had lacked all possibility, all weapons, all communication for struggle. But confronted with an opportunity given them by strangers, most of whom were of the same race as the hated master class, they gave their lives in a moment and apparently without a qualm.

History, even revolutionary history, treats them as fillers-in of blank spaces. Did they simply take the guns and shoot and get shot like so many extras in the movies?

Anderson did not think so.

Although he does not expand upon the facts when he refers to the number of "colored" men killed, his emphasis upon the number is obviously not due just to his racial pride. It must always be borne in mind that he was speaking to a generation to which this incident would conjure up an extremely earth-shaking perspective. And even the slightest emphasis would go a long way.

A DIFFERENT CIVIL WAR

The Civil War may have begun by the time his story was published, but it is clear from the text that it had not begun when he wrote it. It is also clear that he was not thinking of that kind of civil war; he had a different concept of how the war would be fought, who would fight it, and who would lead it.

The war that Anderson had in mind would have required not just a few Black and white guerrillas, no matter how brave and ready to die, but an all-out participation of the slave population, along with a fairly massive support from the North. He must have felt—and with good reason—that this would paralyze the U.S. government (which was already divided between "free soil" and pro-slavery forces) so that especially with Lincoln now president, it would not be able to intervene powerfully on the side of the South, as it had done in the case of Brown's raid.

What actually happened was that the South seceded before such a war could get started and in effect started its own *counter-revolutionary* war. When the fighting erupted, it seemed at first to have very little to do with slavery. The official battle cry in the North was not "Liberate the Slaves," but "Preserve the Union."

Right up until Fort Sumter on April 12, 1861, it must have appeared to Anderson (and many thousands of other passionate Black and white abolitionists in the North) that the Northern capitalist government never would fight. Even after Lincoln's election and even after several states had seceded, it must have appeared that the U.S. government would never wage ruthless war against the slave owners of the South. The formal Confederacy was already established before Lincoln was inaugurated. And Lincoln waited more than a month before he acted. And even then he acted only under the prod of South Carolina's provocative attack on Sumter.

It was, of course, a war against slavery when it did come, regardless of the will of most of its official leaders. In spite of its defects, it was a revolution against the slavocracy that had ruled the whole country. It was a revolution that destroyed forever the power of the slave owners as a class and chattel slavery as a system. But it was a revolution most unsatisfactory to the slaves themselves. The ending of slavery as an institution, as is well known, did not lead to any real amelioration of the actual conditions of life, particularly the economic conditions, for the vast majority of Black people at that time.

What would the conclusion have been if the war had been fought as a revolution from start to finish?

First, the slaves would have been freed simply by striking off their own shackles. Second, they would have enforced their freedom by expropriating the plantations of the masters and dividing up the land. The Thirteenth, Fourteenth, and Fifteenth Amendments, if they took that form, would merely have been legal afterthoughts. The former slaveholders could never have made a comeback of the proportions they actually did, and the whole system of racial inequality that prevails today would have no material basis at all.

We are apt to think of the United States as being *the* capitalist country, as completely money-oriented, Babbittish, nonfeudal, dynamic, etc., etc. But in the more historical sense, it is not so purely capitalist after all.

Probably no bourgeois revolution in history was a completely "finished" one that definitively settled all questions of bourgeois democracy and made social and political conditions thoroughly consistent with bourgeois revolutionary ideas. But the southern United States, and in fact the *whole* United States, in spite of some small and temporary advances during Reconstruction, is to this day a classical example of the most *unfinished* of all bourgeois revolutions. And one of the fundamental reasons for this is that there was no general thoroughgoing slave insurrection, no division of the land.

THE MASTERS WERE COWARDS

Did anybody in the United States fully understand the possibilities of Black insurrection in 1859, not to mention 1861?

Yes. The slave masters understood this. And they understood it so well that they didn't have to write it down or talk about it. In fact, this was probably the subject of their nightly dreams—or nightmares—for years.

Anderson speaks on several occasions about the "cowardice" of the white Virginia aristocracy at Harper's Ferry, including especially among his targets Colonel Lewis Washington, a direct descendent of the "Father of His Country," a title Anderson uses with appropriate irony.

This "cowardice" does not seem to fit with subsequent conduct of most Southern white soldiers—and even officers—in the Civil War. At least, it doesn't fit with the picture we are given in the official history books. But Anderson is not lying, or even exaggerating. He is describing a special class situation and a *class* cowardice in the face of a death-threat to that class.

The slaveholding South, in a certain sense, was much more upset by John Brown's raid than by the beginning of the Civil War itself.

How could twenty Black and white revolutionaries have created so much hysteria, while the organized invasion of massed Northern troops was met by a fervor of militant, self-confident, and even temporarily victorious defensism?

The difference between the John Brown raid and the long-fought Civil War was not just in the massive character of the latter as opposed to the allegedly individualist character of the former. It wasn't just that the Northern army had conventional organization into companies, regiments, brigades, and so on, as opposed to the general guerrilla insurrection almost begun by Brown and Anderson.

The real difference lay in the fact that one conceived of a slave uprising and took the first steps in that direction—while the other, although forced to free the slaves in the long run, and forced to enlist nearly 200,000 Black men in its ranks, did not at first contemplate an actual slave uprising, and, in fact, opposed it.

The alleged bravery of the Southern slaveholders in fighting well-regimented and more or less conventionally organized white Northerners was one thing. The really cowardly panic of these same reactionary individuals when confronted with a direct slave uprising was something else again.

Anderson makes much of this cowardice—but not just to satisfy his well-justified personal hatred of the slave masters. He wanted to assure white Northerners as well as Black that the white South would fall apart in the fires of *real* civil war. The decadent rulers of the South had ruled the country for too long, he was saying. They were a doomed class. And a slave rebellion aided by the progressive North would polish them off in the shortest time.

THE GHOST OF NAT TURNER

No white in the South—and not many in the North—had forgotten the revolt of Nat Turner thirty years earlier. "Small" though it had been, it struck terror into the heart of every single slaveholder. It had spread to many more than its three or four originators within hours after it had broken out. (Like the slaves who took arms from Anderson and the others at Harper's Ferry, the Blacks of Southhampton County did not need a great deal of urging.)

The whole family of the owner of the plantation on which Turner was enslaved was killed in the night. The revolutionaries had decided that they must be completely ruthless at the beginning and kill all whites in their path so that none could give the alarm and they could enlarge their nucleus of an army without being wiped out prematurely.

The shaken masters of the area effected a furious reprisal campaign, killing at least two Blacks for every white who had died. They would have killed far, far more but for the fact that the slaves cost them money. As it was, they must have beaten and tortured thousands. Among other things, they cut off the heads of some of the rebels and posted them at the four corners of at least one village as an example of their vengeance.

It is safe to say that the masters all over the South remembered Nat Turner better than the illiterate and unorganized slaves themselves did. Rulers are nearly always more aware of the dangers of their slaves rebelling than the slaves are. This is because each slave knows only his own heart and is unacquainted with the over-all situation, whereas the masters have all the advantages of communication, travel, information, etc.

These particular rulers hardly needed intelligence reports, however, to tell them they were not loved, not even by the house servants. Whatever their propaganda preachers said to the contrary in the pulpit and the Congress, they knew in their souls that the Blacks might someday rise against them in greater numbers and with greater success than Nat Turner's band.

Thus Anderson was not the only one who was thinking of insurrection. His enemies, the counter-revolutionary slave masters, were desperately afraid of such an event and were thinking of it daily.

And Anderson's friends among the white abolitionists were thinking of it, too. At first they had denied all intention of such a thing. (Brown himself denied it, even in his last defiant speech in the Virginia courtroom, so wicked a thing was such an insurrection considered to be!) But after Brown's raid, more Northerners thought in terms of insurrection.

The redoubtable Thomas Wentworth Higginson, a white minister who took rifles to Kansas and later gave up the cloth to lead a Black regiment in the war, wrote and published a sympathetic sketch of the Nat Turner revolt precisely in 1861, the year the Civil War began and the year of Anderson's present essay. Higginson, too, was obviously thinking of a new slave rebellion on a bigger scale. (He was also one of the "Secret Six," who raised funds for the Harper's Ferry action.)

This was not a case of "Let's you and him fight," either. Higginson had already risked his life several times, most notably in the attempt of several Black and white abolitionists to break into the Boston Court House in 1854 to rescue a captured fugitive slave.

(A deputy U.S. marshal guarding the Black man was killed on that occasion and Higginson, along with others, was accused of the killing. Unlike young Jonathan Jackson, who tried a similar rescue on August 7, 1970, Higginson escaped.)

Even on the Senate floor there were occasional suggestions—after the Civil War had begun and the North was not winning—along the lines of encouraging slave rebellion.

The army of Black soldiers *within the Union lines,* when it was finally formed late in 1862, was in the last analysis, an embodiment of this slave revolution. But it was much less revolutionary than what Brown and Anderson had in mind.

The Black regiments were revolutionary in that they struggled against their own and their relatives' slavery. But their creation and existence was also a subordination of the Black freedom struggle to the discipline of the anti-slavemaster capitalist class. It was a subordination of the revolutionary Black soldier to the moderate or often only half-revolutionary white Northern officer.

BLACK-WHITE GUERRILLA ARMY IN THE SOUTH?

But of course Anderson was not thinking of this kind of revolution in the first place. (As a matter of fact most of the abolitionists in the North—Black as well as white—had been thinking along the lines of *Northern* secession from the Union.) Anderson was completely sympathetic to Nat Turner with respect to his attitude toward insurrection and toward ruthlessness against the masters. He is critical of Brown—in the present essay—for the latter's last-minute softness with prisoners. But he visualized the coming revolution as one of the Harper's Ferry type rather than that of Southhampton County.

He felt that the slaves would rise up with the moral aid of fighters like Brown and himself to inspire them and with material aid of rifles and other supplies to arm them. And these would come from the North.

In the actual Civil War, the slaves were discouraged from rising up behind the lines, when Lincoln countermanded his own more abolition-minded generals and ordered that escaping slaves be sent back to the tender mercies of their masters. This went on for more than a year. After that, it was little less than amazing that hundreds of thousands of Black soldiers still joined the fight by enlisting in the Union Army. The only explanation is that the revolutionary need was so great and the faith that freedom would come was so deep.

Anderson knew that the slaves could not get enough weapons by themselves or establish communications on a statewide, much less countrywide basis. He knew the masters had the railroad and telegraph, which they had not had in Nat Turner's time. But he also knew that Northern whites had more railroads and better telegraphs. Northern whites were much more familiar with these and other modern inventions than the white masters of the South. He knew that if the Northerners came down and joined the slave rebellion, they would add the necessary strength and technique to insure the victory.

In Anderson's concept, Harper's Ferry was a Black-white military alliance against slavery and was in no sense an episodic display of white altruism, any more than it was one of Black madness.

In the very beginning of his book he broadly hints that other attempts like Brown's, other plans to "invade" the South, were in the works. So he probably knew of three or four Harper's Ferry-type raids being planned and was no doubt personally acquainted with fifty to a hundred whites whom he considered reliable enough and revolutionary enough to do this.

Being a rational person, however, he must also have had a perspective of where to go from there. He must have known as well as anybody else, after his experiences at the Ferry, that neither a hundred nor a thousand whites, even with extra rifles to pass around, would be enough to win the revolution. He must have conceived, therefore, of a much larger struggle, although along the same general lines. He must have had some reason to suppose that many thousands of whites would come down South and join with the hundreds of thousands of Blacks in the revolution.

But how would the necessary thousands of whites be induced to do this? Assuming that the Blacks would go into the swamps, the hills, and the forests in sufficient numbers to set up a formidable guerrilla army, who would recruit the large numbers of Northern whites to bring the guns, and what battle cry would bring them down to risk their lives in such a fight?

It is true that it never did happen in just this way. But, just to take Anderson's suppositions, would it have been *possible* to recruit the whites for this kind of war? Could such a war have come about, for example, if the Northern capitalists had waited still longer—as they certainly *wanted* to wait—before declaring war on the South?

LAND AND THE WHITE NORTH

There were great and compelling reasons why the average poor or middle-class Northerner, who was not usually an abolitionist, should struggle against the slave owners.

One of the greatest reasons was the yearning for free land in the West.

Apparently this land was "free" to any white who killed enough of the Indians who lived on it and "owned" it, if anybody did. But the reality was that it was never even that free. The slave owners were determined to get this land, keep it for themselves, and not permit any general emigration to the West. The Northern railroad capitalists were also determined to get it. But they had an interest in supporting, for a time, the aspirations of the would-be small farmers. When bills came up in Congress for a Homestead Act, the "railroad congressmen" always voted for them, while the Southern representatives voted against them.

Naturally, those whites ready to take up arms to imitate the action of John Brown would have had to be made of heroic stuff and not just be land-seekers with their individual minds bent on plowing, seeding, and cultivating. They would have had to be ready to give up their lives for their fellow human beings—the other land seekers and the slaves.

But where would such people come from? Would they simply arise from the ground? Could there have been a dozen John Browns or a hundred or a thousand?

Yes. The land problem would, by pressing upon the consciousness of a whole generation in the North, also produce heroism in the struggle against the slaveholders and empathy for Black rebellion in the minds of millions of whites. In fact, it had already done so.

UNCLE TOM FANNED THE FLAMES

One sign of this was the phenomenal popularity of *Uncle Tom's Cabin*. It was by far the most popular novel of the century. Whatever misconceptions the book may have had about the Black character as personified by Uncle Tom, it certainly did appeal to the sympathies of the Northern whites and fanned the flames for the fight against slavery.

The abolitionists, including Brown and Anderson, had been fighting for many years before *Uncle Tom's Cabin* came on the scene in 1852. But they had been a tiny minority. The Fugitive Slave Law of 1850, along with the virtual repeal of the Missouri Compromise—which appeared to close off Western land from small-family settlement—made a mighty impact upon the people. The advent of *Uncle Tom's Cabin* coincided with the social impact of these events.

And it is worth noting that the great protest novel was not written about the land in the West but about the oppression in the South. This was not due to any deviousness on the part of Harriet Beecher Stowe; it was due to her genuine sympathy for other human beings.

But this sympathy did coincide with the Northern white land hunger for the West.

For the first time in America large numbers of whites identified with the perils of a Black heroine. Eliza escaping her master and crossing the moving ice with her baby in her arms later became the cliché of the century. But it was a burning reality at the time. Familiar as such harrowing stories were to the Black slaves, this was a brand-new concept and a universal political thesis to millions of free Northern whites.

Before *Uncle Tom's Cabin* the whites' image of the Black slave was that of a subhuman being. The book, in spite of what seems like mere sentimentalism today, made a revolutionary transformation of that image.

In the light of today's racism, the word "subhuman" may seem to be merely a vicious figure of speech. But at that time this was a literal concept and actual belief of the super-brainwashed whites. This appalling ignorance was just as synthetically created by ruling-class propaganda as today's racism is, of course. But it had to be more extreme in order to justify the more extreme torture and degradation of Black people.

There were sober arguments over whether Black people had a soul, for instance. And even among more friendly whites there were discussions about "natural" laziness, "natural" talent for music and dancing, and whether Black people could possibly be taught the ABC's, etc., ad nauseam. Even the brave Higginson does this again and again in his book *Army Life in a Black Regiment.*[15]

The picture of the fervently praying Uncle Tom who forgave his enemies in such a good Christian way supplied a new and at the same time relatively superior image of the slave—an image that many Northern whites, suckled on Victorian Christianity, would fight for, and some would die for.

---

[15] Thomas Wentworth Higginson, *Army Life in a Black Regiment* (Boston: Beacon Press, 1962).

"Uncle Tom" has a totally different meaning today, of course. And we should not quarrel with history over the fact that this long-dead image is useless for today's tasks.

At the same time, however, we should understand that many whites did die for old Uncle Tom, and he did serve his purpose for the idealism of the white ally, if not for the soldierly passion of the Black revolutionary. (The latter hardly needed a novel to explain about Simon Legree and the sting of the whip!)

Thus, in the social soil of white land hunger and hatred for the slave-owning land monopolists, there grew up the plant of white people's anti-slavery and here and there the flower of personal dedication to struggle unto death against it.

Brown himself, awakening to the struggle long before the publication of *Uncle Tom's Cabin*, had planned the Harper's Ferry action for at least a decade and perhaps a quarter of a century. His feat in turn had an even more profound effect upon Northern feeling than Stowe's very successful book (which also helped prepare the masses to more fully appreciate Brown's action).

Having said all this, it is no putdown to say that the genuine mass hero-worship for Brown's majestic self-sacrifice, like the sentimental sympathy for Uncle Tom, was closely connected to and deeply rooted in the Northern drive for land in the West.

LAND AND THE BLACK-WHITE SOUTH

Thus Anderson had good reason to count on help from the whites of the North. In the actual event of the Civil War, hundreds of thousands of young Northern farmers and city workers—often whole union locals of them—enlisted en masse in the Union Army with conscious and final commitment to the fight against slavery.

But Anderson, perhaps unbeknown to himself at the time he wrote this book, had an even more powerful lever—the land question in the South itself.

A tiny oligarchy owned the bulk of the land, just as it owned the bulk of the slaves.

But the idea of giving land to the Black landless was never mentioned in the North before the Civil War. And it is possible that neither Anderson nor Brown had considered the idea of dividing up the plantations among the slaves—although this would seem to be a likely enough concept, and not one to frighten men who were already risking so much for freedom.

The slaves themselves, so far as is known, did not raise the demand for land at this time, either. Many factors prevented them from being able to do this. But they surely would have accepted the idea, just as quickly and logically as they accepted guns at Harper's Ferry, particularly in the course of any extended struggle against the great landowners.

The very logic of slave revolt would inevitably lead to the division of the land. The *occupation* of the land by an army of rebellious slaves would almost dictate it.

And what about the poor whites—in the Southern countryside? The "squatters" who lived on the fringes of the big plantations, as well as hundreds of thousands of impoverished small white landholders and tenant farmers in the less fertile areas—they, too, needed land.

These whites—who did not get land and later became soldiers in the Confederate Army—were already more or less experienced in independent farming. They would have been even more receptive than the slaves to the idea of division of the plantations and to title to the backlands.

If Lincoln had made the Proclamation of Emancipation on April 12, 1861, instead of on January 1, 1863, the Civil War would have been much more thorough and probably much shorter—because the slave rebellion would have been immediate and continuous.

But if Osborne Anderson and his friends had also on the same date made a proclamation that the plantations were to be divided among the slaves, with land also being provided for the white "squatters," and if they had made the proclamation from an army headquarters, guerrilla or otherwise, what a different Civil War that would have been and what a different South the South would now be!

The masters would not have had a single reliable slave behind their lines. And the poor whites would have seen the Black slaves as their greatest allies. Regardless of the racist past, they would have fought side by side with the slaves to overthrow the masters.

This great solidarity would not by itself have eliminated racism. But this, *combined* with the division of the land and creation of a more or less equal Black-white yeomanry, would have changed the course of all subjective opinions and attitudes along with the objective course of U.S. history itself.

The consequent new farmers of the South would have not only conquered slave owners who were holding back the Northern capitalists from building railroads, etc., they would also have created a tremendous new market for Northern capital, such as the West later provided.

Why did the capitalists of the North not welcome such a development and not bend their efforts to hasten it along?

Why did the great political leaders of the North—with only a couple of exceptions—close their eyes to this whole perspective? Why did they not even raise the idea or put it into words before or during the war? Why did they, in effect, sabotage their own revolution?

THEY FEARED THEIR OWN REVOLUTION

It is generally understood nowadays that Lincoln waited so long to make the Emancipation Proclamation because he hoped for the capitulation of the slave owners without it—that is, he hoped to convince them that he was not revolutionary and would not touch their property in slaves.

That is quite true and it is a true measure of the general capitalist reluctance to fight the slave owners in the first place. It was the capitalist system that compelled them to fight rather than capitalist ideals, or even necessarily each individual capitalist's individual interests. It was the irresistible drive of capital into the West and the equally desperate drive of the slave system to move its cotton production westward that had come into the kind of collision that involved the big capitalists on the side of the revolution.

In this situation, Lincoln had the same motives with respect to the land that he had with respect to the slaves. Both were *property*.

The division of the land, like the freeing of the slaves, would have been part of the classical capitalist revolution (such as in France in 1789). And particularly in land-rich America, it should have been the most "natural" thing in the world.

But it wasn't.

The capitalists feared nothing so much as their own revolution—the revolution that was to put them into power over unprecedented wealth and natural resources. They feared it because they questioned their ability to control it.

To take the Western lands from the Native people, difficult and bloody as that task was, involved no blood-letting *within their own system*, and raised no threat at all to their own property.

But to expropriate the land of the slave owners (many of whom had financial ties to the merchant capital, etc., in the North) was also to question the legality of *all* huge land ownership. And at this very moment the big capitalists, especially the railroad companies, were getting land by the millions of acres from Congress, swindling the white masses as well as the Indians in the process.

The most radical political representatives of the capitalists in Congress did propose the "forty acres and a mule" division of the land, *after the war*, during the Reconstruction. But the majority of Congress never did support that, and in the absence of an active political alliance of a substantial number of whites, the freed slaves were not able to effect this division for themselves.[*]

From the beginning, the capitalists preferred a compromise with the slave masters at the expense of the slaves. But when this proved

---

[*] After the war, the Black people did fight—magnificently—for the land whenever the opportunity arose and the arms were available, especially between 1868 and 1872 (height of Reconstruction). But the "war" was then over and the white plebeian alliance was by this time exhausted, while all the "radicalism" of the left Republicans in Congress really amounted to was to use the Blacks virtually *alone* to put the finishing touches on the crushing of the *national* power of the Southern white landlords.

impossible and the capitalists were absolutely *forced* into a revolution, they got into a position to control the revolution and bend it completely to their own needs.

They moderated the revolution, even while they extended its scope and threw more tremendous forces into it. They could not succeed in their original intention, which was to leave slavery untouched in the South and merely prevent its extension into the West. But they were able to make their peace with the former slaveholders after Reconstruction and give them back the mastery of the South as agents and partners of the capitalist North. Most important, they helped the Southern masters cheat the freed slaves out of the land—out of those "forty acres and a mule" that the more radical capitalist politicians had promised the slaves during Reconstruction.

Anderson could not be expected to foresee this betrayal, especially in light of the fact that the capitalists themselves did not foresee it—any more than they foresaw their own reluctant half-decision to begin giving the Blacks the land in the first place.

But the successful division of the Southern land, accompanied by the guerrilla warfare that must have been envisioned by Anderson and Brown—that is, the arming of the masses—would have thwarted the betrayal of 1877, or made it nine-tenths ineffective. So whatever social and political understanding Anderson and Brown may have lacked, it would have been more than made up for by their military program, could that have been put into practice.

GOD—AND THE GOD OF BATTLE

Anderson's story is couched in the literary style then fashionable, with references to religious concepts, etc. He himself most likely shared Brown's and Harriet Beecher Stowe's feeling about a God of Vengeance that worked through devoted human beings his wonders to perform. But his motivations were not nearly as religious as the sentiments expressed in the book might lead a modern revolutionary to suppose.

Considering that he was so strong for new attempts along the same lines as Harper's Ferry, it is clear that he had no faith that the

Jericho walls of prejudice and slavery would have simply crumbled to pieces at old Brown's great trumpet blast. He must have taken for granted what Brown seemed to discover only at the end:

"I, John Brown, am now quite certain that the crimes of this guilty land will never be purged away but with Blood."

People like Henry David Thoreau and Emerson hailed Brown as the man whose self-sacrifice would ennoble and transform white humanity—almost in the literal sense. That is, they did not then see the action as valuable in the sense of being a concrete beginning of a broad military struggle, so much as they saw the "transcendental" aspect and a new redemption of Man—with a capital M.

But Anderson and the more active abolitionists saw Brown's execution and the popular indignation as the point of departure for new military thrusts rather than for any particular moral regeneration. This is concealed somewhat in Anderson's text, perhaps because of his own religious beliefs and undoubtedly because of his own deep respect for Brown's powerful convictions.

He does mention Brown's leading the prayers at the farmhouse headquarters, but he doesn't repeat them. He tends to emphasize, rather, Brown's complete lack of racist prejudice, his stern, fair leadership and his mercy, mixed with terrible swift justice. And much as he is prone to religious sentiments himself, Anderson does not repeat any of Brown's statements about "God's children," etc.

On the other hand, this was partly because he was talking to people already as familiar with Brown's famous words as they were with the Twenty-third Psalm or the Lord's Prayer.

The following excerpt from Brown's speech to the Virginia court had already been printed and reprinted throughout the North by the time Anderson wrote his book.

This court acknowledges, I suppose, the validity of the law of God. I see a book kissed here which I suppose to be the Bible, or at least the New Testament. That teaches me that all things whatsoever I would that men should do to me, I should do even so to them. It teaches me further, "to remember them that are in bonds as bound with them." I endeavored to act up to that instruction. I say, I am yet too young to understand that God is any respecter of persons. I believe that to have interfered as I have done—as I have always freely admitted to have done—in behalf of his despised poor, was not wrong, but right. Now, if it is deemed necessary that I should forfeit my life for the furtherance of the ends of justice and mingle my blood further with the blood of my children and with the blood of millions in this slave country whose rights are disregarded by wicked, cruel, and unjust enactments—I submit; so let it be done!

One can imagine the young men and women of the North reading those words by whale-oil lamp and candle, along with the anti-slavery poems of James Russell Lowell and John Greenleaf Whittier and the stories of Harriet Beecher Stowe. Given the form of the national crisis, they must have been literally pressing at the leash of social restraint.

Brown's simple, powerful words, "I think I cannot now better serve the cause I love so much than to die for it"—these words so inspired the white North that they were painted on banners and hung across the streets of Cleveland, Ohio (Brown's adopted state) after his execution.

It was not more inspiration that the more revolutionary of the white Northern youth needed now; it was organization and a *plan*.

TO STRIKE THE RED-HOT IRON

Naturally Anderson's plans were military rather than political: But it was precisely a military blow that was needed. The land question in the South, like the land question in the West, was bursting to be answered in the actual blow for Black freedom. Like Brown's, Anderson's mind was fixed on freedom itself and on the plans for the military action to get it. And instead of seeing great social and economic questions as fundamental to this freedom, he may have seen them as derivative at best, or have taken them for granted.

The military blow, or more precisely, the *idea* and *example* of that blow was the great contribution that the band had already made and the contribution that Anderson and others were preparing to make again. In a revolutionary epoch it is the action itself that counts, more than the theory about it—although it is painfully true that even then, without a correct theory, without an adequate over-all plan, much, if not all, can be lost.

Thus, it is only on the question of military procedure that Anderson makes any criticism of Brown, in spite of his high regard for him. He scores Brown's over-sensitivity about the prisoners and especially his unnecessary delay in retreating into the hills.

It is very possible that the old captain made important tactical errors. He himself admitted one or two of them to his captors. And it is also possible that he was more aware than Anderson of the hopelessness of a general retreat at the time.

But Anderson's insistence on his point about the tactics shows his eagerness to win the actual military struggle and his supreme confidence that the slaves would join the enlarged fight he had in mind. In this he may well have been more perceptive than Brown and more in tune with the possibilities for a more revolutionary civil war.

REALISM AND REVOLUTION

It is hard to prove the possibilities of that which did not happen. It is hard to prove just how realistic Anderson was in his revolutionary optimism.

But the practicality of his outlook is contained, in the last analysis, in the realism of the Harper's Ferry venture itself.

For nearly a hundred years John Brown's feat was viewed as that of an adventurer, a madman, a "putschist." But that was because people had forgotten the old revolution and could not conceive of a new one.

At the time of Harper's Ferry, or shortly thereafter, Brown was regarded as a great leader, a sterling revolutionary, and even something of a saint. (Anderson himself puts Brown partially into the latter category.) And now,[*] after decades of slander as a madman, Brown is again regarded as a great revolutionary and the Harper's Ferry "raid" is again considered a realistic and logically planned act as well as a heroic one.

This is because our age is beginning to duplicate some of the conditions of the pre-Civil War period and today's social situation is be-

---

[*] This introduction was written in 1974 for the first edition of this book.

ginning to produce new social thinkers and doers. Our minds are flowering in a different social soil than the minds of our conservative parents and grandparents. The needs of the oppressed are seen by more and more people as requiring a revolutionary solution.

But even in revolutions, the human mind is the last thing to be revolutionized. At the beginning of every new war the generals try to fight the old war. And revolutions of olden times are revived in the mind before the revolution of the new times takes full shape and before the new mental leap is actually made to the full requirements of the present.

So it was that George Washington, John Adams, and the others established the ancient Roman "Senatus." So it was that John Brown and Osborne Anderson saw themselves and the slaves as the reincarnation of the Chosen People and viewed the nineteenth-century Southern masters as though they were ancient Egyptians who would surely be visited by plague and pestilence for their sins.

Similarly, many heroes of our own time often look for the form of their revolution in the past, even though the essence of it is in the present. And sometimes they think they are the reincarnation of John Brown or Nat Turner. Indeed, there are few better examples of revolutionary heroism to imitate than the kind Brown's band displayed— if the feat is correctly understood and evaluated. But this can only be done in the light of modern revolutionary theory and international experience—that is, genuine Marxism-Leninism.

The greatest mistakes in judging the Harper's Ferry raid usually flow from the assumption that Brown and the others were "individualists" in the bourgeois or anarchist sense, and that besides seeing themselves as the elect of God, they saw *nobody else as elect,* and didn't conceive of a countrywide revolution.

This assumption shows a total misunderstanding of both the men and the times.

It should be clearly understood that an isolated act, unrelated to the needs or the consciousness of the masses, cannot in any sense be regarded as revolutionary. Even in a generally revolutionary period it is usually wrong for the conscious revolutionaries to *substitute* themselves for the masses and expect to win freedom for them without their participation.

But this was not at all the intention of Brown or any of the band.

The realism of the action was proven not only by the alacrity of the slaves in accepting weapons and risking their lives for freedom with hardly a moment to think it over; not only by the tremendous wave of sympathy for Brown and his men that swept the country—and indeed half the world—but also by the fact that substantial numbers of regular armed U.S. troops were required to put out the fires of revolt at Harper's Ferry itself.

It was truly symbolic that Colonel Washington, the descendant of the "Father of his Country," had to give up the original Washington's distinguished sword to Black Osborne Anderson.

But it was more than symbolic that Robert E. Lee, the future general of the whole Confederate Army, and his lieutenant, J. E. B. Stuart, had to lead the counter-revolutionary U.S. troops against this "little," apparently minuscule, revolt.

Had the band lacked support among the people—i.e., the Black people—it would have taken hardly more than a police or possibly a militia action to put them down.

The group's crack shooting certainly did frighten the pro-slavery white populace fully as much as Anderson thought. But the fact that *slaves* were shooting, too, frightened them still more. Three thousand U.S. troops stood by when Brown and his companions were hanged a few weeks later. They were not serving as an honor guard, but as a grim warning to the restless freedom-yearning slaves.

THE STRUGGLE THIS TIME

In speaking of certain deeper social-psychological problems, Thomas Wolfe said, "You can't go home again." And that proposition is a hundred times more true for society itself than for the individual.

Neither white nor Black; neither farmworker, farm tenant, small owner, nor anyone else is going back to 1859 or 1861 to fight the Civil War as it should have been fought.

The idea of individual families trying to make a living on forty acres of average farmland today would be hopelessly reactionary. It would condemn them to lifetime poverty. It would be a "Tobacco Road" society for everybody.

The great big estates still have to be expropriated, but not now by the riflemen of Nat Turner or John Brown. It is the immense North-South agribankers owning the million-acre farms, forests, and plantations who have to be ousted now, but no longer to make way for a couple of million Black-white dirt farmers. Now the problem is to make the huge factories-in-the-fields produce for everybody and be owned by everybody (except the present bank-owners who are entirely parasitic, useless and—being exploiters—worse than useless).

To rise up in Southhampton County was not enough even then; to rise up at Harper's Ferry was not enough even then; the whole Civil War was not enough to bring about the division of the land—to bring about the capitalist ideal of each family being its own independent production unit. The "free farm" of song and story never really did exist in this country after the Civil War, and never even superficially existed for the Black people. And now the productive system has far surpassed the small farm economy.

Where the material basis for Black freedom once lay in the small, independently owned farm, it now lies in another direction entirely.

Now the struggle is one against the same big business that defeated the Southern landlords, the same big business that is now both landlord-banker and factory lord. Now the struggle is no longer to become a little capitalist in partnership with the big capitalists. Now the struggle is to eliminate the capitalists altogether.

And just as every military move of Brown and Anderson tended inevitably to strengthen some progressive aspect of capitalism against the slave system, so the actual struggle of working people against the corporations today tends to strengthen the forces of socialism and prepare the way for the socialist revolution.

But again, this does not mean that the fight will follow the precise path that rational logic may predetermine for it.

Because white racism is so prevalent and powerful, it is still possible that some new phase of the Black liberation struggle will arise and the Black masses will fight for an entirely separate national development. It is possible that the idea of Black sovereignty and the concept of the Black republic will become the main moving slogans for the Black people.

If so, these slogans will be profoundly revolutionary even *if* they temporarily revive the idea of small independent farms again. This is because the anti-imperialist aspect of the matter will be the dominant aspect. And what begins as an abstractly capitalist Black republic will most probably end concretely as a socialist one.

But *whether or not* there is a powerful Black separatist movement, the question of Black-white unity against big business still remains fundamental.

How, for example, will *either* Black or white be able to conquer the common corporate oppressor in the face of ugly, disunifying white racism?

The white workers will overcome their racism—just as surely as their ancestors overcame their belief in leprechauns, goblins, and witches. But this may be a long process for most of them, far too long, considering the urgency of the fight and the vital need for early unity against a much more powerful and dangerous oppressor than the Southern slave masters.

Most likely the curse of racism will only be completely washed away some time *after* the racist ruling class is defeated and the instruments of education are taken over by the revolutionary class. Perhaps only a new generation of children, brought up in the love and equality established by the truly human family—in the true family of humanity—will be really free of racism.

Among those thousands of whites who died for Black freedom in the Civil War, there were very few who were entirely free of racist attitudes of one kind or another. In their own minds they were dying for the white-sentimentalist image of Uncle Tom or Topsy, rather than for the real living children of Nat Turner. And it is possible that many of them were guilty of much worse conceptions, and even actions, than this.

But the totally pure in heart seldom get into revolutions. And even the most dedicated individual revolutionaries seldom prevail upon the revolutionary masses to live up to the revolutionary ideal in all respects, even when the latter are in the process of creating the basis for a wholly new and different society.

Just as the mass of people do not generally support the revolution until they have already *made* the revolution, so the white masses will most probably fight against racism in society long before they have conquered it in their own minds.

With the cadres and real leaders of revolution, it is of course different. On the one hand, people fight for the future when their minds are still mired in the past. On the other hand, individual heroes catch a glimpse of the future long before it begins and before the open struggle breaks out. And they battle for the *minds* of the vanguard.

What made the Harper's Ferry group so unlike but yet so like the rest of their generation was the fact that they did what they did in relative isolation, but they did it as an advance scouting party of those millions who were to fight on the battlefields of the Civil War.

They did it against the social pressure and legal barriers of the day. And yet at the same time they expressed the subconscious feelings of the millions. It was their sublime *struggle*, needless to add, that raised these mass feelings from the subconscious to the conscious.

It was their confidence in oppressed humanity's ability to end its oppression that gave them the ability to sacrifice themselves under the conditions they did.

The *religious form* that some of them, especially Brown himself, gave to this confidence had little to do with their own real motivations or their rational—and therefore *real*—vision of freedom. Their faith in the Christian God was only a symbolic expression of their belief in *people*.

And the people—that is, the revolutionary generation—did fight, and on the most colossal scale. They did not fight in exactly the way

Anderson and Brown hoped they would fight. But they fought hard and long and they did destroy the institution of chattel slavery.

By clearing the field of this ancient evil they laid the basis for the modern struggle against the modern evils.

The fact that this modern struggle, the fight for socialism, is a long time coming, the fact that it must overcome mountains of miseducation, ruling-class racism and deceit, obscures, just as the pre-Civil War official philosophy and racism did, the inevitability of the coming revolution. It obscures the absolutely irreconcilable character of the *class* antagonisms that will and must be fought through to the end.

The class antagonisms of today are very different from those of 1859 and 1861. The struggle this time will be led by the oppressed themselves—that is by the Browns and the Andersons of the proletariat rather than by the Lincolns and Grants of the bourgeoisie. Where the heroes of Harper's Ferry failed to effect the kind of revolution they wanted, their descendants will succeed.

WHO WILL BRING THE GUNS THIS TIME?

It is hard to predict the course of a new revolution, which, like a newly rampaging mountain river cutting into different terrain than before, flows most logically and "naturally" in what later seems to have been a predetermined course. Yet at the same time it astounds all its beholders with its elemental fury, power, and suddenness.

The unfinished old revolution cannot but have a very powerful and profound effect upon the still-unperceived new one. And we ought to try to understand what that effect will be.

The living river of that old revolution is the Black people, who have been forced to leave the countryside and come into the city and the factory. And that river will most probably burst from underground, so to speak, into *another* river of revolt by both Black and white.

The Black workers are already bringing more class consciousness and class struggle into the plants along with national consciousness and the struggle for racial equality. The national feeling and the necessity for struggle as an oppressed nation are residues from the old revolution begun by Anderson, Turner, Brown, and the others—the revolution that was never finished.

The Black workers are still fighting that old revolution—not in the romantic sense of imagining themselves still at Harper's Ferry, but in the all-too-real sense of still fighting against nineteenth-century type oppression. They are still fighting the old revolution, and in doing so, they are preparing themselves to be leaders of the new one.

The white workers, on the other hand, will at a certain point be as desperately in need of the new revolution as the Black workers have been in need of the old one all along. The most brilliant and daring leaders of the Blacks will at that point also learn how to get the confidence of the whites.

This does not necessarily mean that the leaders of the Black-white working class will all be Black. But it does mean that the Black penetration of the North today, like the white penetration of the South yesterday, will lead to the most revolutionary results. And this time, due to the similar status of both of these groups within the working class (relative to their exploiters), due to the completely counter-revolutionary status of the capitalist class that now exploits both North and South, due to the fact that the coming crisis will hit both Black and white workers with great severity, the revolution will be fought through to the end.

For the present historical moment, it is true, the white majority is still listening to the banalities and the bestialities of the now thoroughly degenerate, outlived capitalist class. But they will begin the great struggle in spite of this. And at some point in that struggle they will turn in another direction altogether and listen to the Black and white revolutionaries of the working class.

They will then learn that history has its lessons, even in the United States. And they will listen with rapt attention to the long unheard and too long unheeded voice from Harper's Ferry.

A VOICE FROM HARPER'S FERRY.

A

NARRATIVE OF EVENTS

AT

HARPER'S FERRY;

WITH

INCIDENTS PRIOR AND SUBSEQUENT TO ITS CAPTURE BY
CAPTAIN BROWN AND HIS MEN.

BY

OSBORNE P. ANDERSON,

ONE OF THE NUMBER.

BOSTON:
PRINTED FOR THE AUTHOR.
1861.

Lewis Sheridan Leary became part of John Brown's band several months before the raid on Harper's Ferry. He was killed at the rifle works. He counted among his ancestors Africans brought to America in chains, a Native person from North Carolina, and an Irish-American Revolutionary War soldier.

Dangerfield Newby had only recently won his freedom from slavery when he was shot dead outside the arsenal gate. His wife and seven children were still enslaved. His comrades remarked on his huge size—six feet, two inches tall.

Shields Green was recommended to Brown by abolitionist leader Frederick Douglass. He was a fugitive slave who had to leave his son in South Carolina. He was tried and hanged for his role in the raid. Anderson called him "the most inexorable of all our party . . . a braver man never lived than Shields Green."

John Brown had led the anti-slavery movement in Kansas before planning the Harper's Ferry attack. Anderson said that "the opinion common among my people" was that the liberator of Kansas was "eminently worthy of the highest veneration."

John Anthony Copeland, Jr., was Leary's cousin and recruited by him. Copeland was an Oberlin student who had served time in jail for helping a fugitive slave. He also was hanged for his role at Harper's Ferry.

In the Civil War in Kansas (1856-1857), white workers and farmers fought alongside escaped slaves. They were resisting invading mercenaries who had been hired by Southern plantation owners trying to impose slavery on the territory.

In 1855 Ann Wood and other Black teenagers escaped from slavery in Virginia and headed North. Here, they fight off an armed posse of slave catchers in Virginia. The group reached Philadelphia safely.

In 1851 a Negro Vigilance Committee in Christiana, Pennsylvania, fought off a posse that had come to claim two runaway slaves. In other incidents, Black and white abolitionists broke into jails and attacked U.S. marshals about to return freed slaves to their masters.

Harriet Tubman, left, with some of the 300 escaped slaves she led to freedom on the Underground Railroad.

After the plantation of Confederate General Drayton was occupied by
Northern troops, freed slaves took it over. Here, they gin cotton.

In 1865 the 107th U.S. Colored Troops from Fort Corcoran were assigned
to guard the capital in Washington, D.C.

Black troops in North Carolina liberate slaves.

Black U.S. Congressperson Robert Brown speaks in favor of a Civil Rights Bill, which was passed in 1875, during Reconstruction. But the Supreme Court declared it "unconstitutional" in 1883.

Cartoon shows President Andrew Johnson making
false promises to a Black Civil War veteran.
Johnson withdrew Union troops from the South,
allowing racist bands to massacre Black people.

OSBORNE P. ANDERSON'S
ANDERSON'S
Narrative

Osborne Perry Anderson was a freedman and a
printer by trade. He escaped after the raid and
lived to fight again, this time as a noncommissioned
officer of the Union in the Civil War.

PREFACE

My sole purpose in publishing the following Narrative is to save from oblivion the facts connected with one of the most important movements of this age, with reference to the overthrow of American slavery. My own personal experience in it, under the orders of Captain Brown, on the 16th and 17th of October, 1859, as the only man alive who was at Harper's Ferry during the entire time—the unsuccessful groping after these facts, by individuals, impossible to be obtained, except from an actor in the scene—and the conviction that the cause of impartial liberty requires this duty at my hands—alone have been the motives for writing and circulating the little book herewith presented.

I will not, under such circumstances, insult nor burden the intelligent with excuses for defects in composition, nor for the attempt to give the facts. A plain, unadorned, truthful story is wanted, and that by one who knows what he says, who is known to have been at the great encounter, and to have labored in shaping the same. My identity as a member of Captain Brown's company cannot be questioned, successfully, by any who are bent upon suppressing the truth; neither will it be by any in Canada or the United States familiar with John Brown and his plans; as those know his men personally, or by reputation, who enjoyed his confidence sufficiently to know thoroughly his plans.

The readers of this narrative will therefore keep steadily in view the main point—that they are perusing a story of events which have happened under the eye of the great Captain, or are incidental thereto, and not a compendium of the "plans" of Captain Brown; for as his plans were not consummated, and as their fulfillment is committed to the future, no one to whom they are known will recklessly expose all of them to the public gaze. Much has been given as true that never happened; much has been omitted that should have been made known; many things have been left unsaid, because, up to within a short time, but two could say them; one of them has been offered up, a sacrifice to the Moloch, Slavery; being that other one, I propose to perform the duty, trusting to that portion of the public who love the right for an appreciation of my endeavor.

O.P.A.

CHAPTER I

The Idea and Its Exponents—John Brown Another Moses

The idea underlying the outbreak at Harper's Ferry is not peculiar to that movement, but dates back to a period very far beyond the memory of the "oldest inhabitant," and emanated from a source much superior to the Wises and Hunters, the Buchanans and Masons of today. It was the appointed work for life of an ancient patriarch spoken of in Exodus, chap. ii., and who, true to his great commission, failed not to trouble the conscience and to disturb the repose of the Pharaohs of Egypt with that inexorable, "Thus saith the Lord: Let my people go!" until even they were urgent upon the people in its behalf. Coming down through the nations, and regardless of national boundaries or peculiarities, it has been proclaimed and enforced by the patriarch and the warrior of the Old World, by the enfranchised freeman and the humble slave of the New.

Its nationality is universal; its language everywhere understood by the haters of tyranny; and those that accept its mission, everywhere understand each other. There is an unbroken chain of sentiment and purpose from Moses of the Jews to John Brown of America; from Kossuth, and the liberators of France and Italy, to the untutored Gabriel, and the Denmark Veseys, Nat Turners and Madison Washingtons of the Southern American States.

The shaping and expressing of a thought for freedom takes the same consistence with the colored American—whether he be an independent citizen of the Haitian nation, a proscribed but humble nominally free colored man, a patient, toiling, but hopeful slave—as with the proudest or noblest representative of European or American civilization and Christianity.

Lafayette, the exponent of French honor and political integrity, and John Brown, foremost among the men of the New World in high moral and religious principle and magnanimous bravery, embrace as brothers of the same mother, in harmony upon the grand mission of liberty; but, while the Frenchman entered the lists in obedience to a desire to aid, and by invitation from the Adamses and Hamiltons, and thus pushed on the political fortunes of those able to help themselves, John Brown, the liberator of Kansas, the projector and commander of the Harper's Ferry expedition, saw in the most degraded slave a man and a brother, whose appeal for his God ordained rights no one should disregard; in the toddling slave child, a captive whose release is as imperative, and whose prerogative is as weighty, as the most famous in the land.

When the Egyptian pressed hard upon the Hebrew, Moses slew him; and when the spirit of slavery invaded the fair Territory of Kansas, causing the Free-State settlers to cry out because of persecution, old John Brown, famous among the men of God forever, though then but little known to his fellow-men, called together his sons and went over, as did Abraham, to the unequal contest, but on the side of the oppressed white men of Kansas that were, and the black men that were to be. Today, Kansas is free, and the verdict of impartial men is, that to John Brown, more than any other man, Kansas owes her present position.

I am not the biographer of John Brown, but I can be indulged in giving here the opinion common among my people of one so eminently worthy of the highest veneration. Close observation of him, during many weeks, and under his orders at his Kennedy Farm fireside, also, satisfies me that in comparing the noble old man to Moses, and other men of piety and renown, who were chosen by God to his great work, none have been more faithful, none have given a brighter record.

CHAPTER II

Preliminaries to Insurrection—What May Be Told and What Not—John Brown's First Visit to Chatham—Some of the Secrets from the "Carpetbag"

To go into particulars, and to detail reports current more than a year before the outbreak, among the many on the United States and Canada who had an inkling of some "practical work" to be done by "Osawatomie Brown," when there should be nothing to do in Kansas—to give facts in that connection, would only forestall future action, without really benefiting the slave, or winning over to that sort of work the anti-slavery men who do not favor physical resistance to slavery.

Slaveholders alone might reap benefits; and for one, I shall throw none in their way, by any indiscreet avowals; they already enjoy more than their share; but to a clear understanding of all the facts to be here published, it may be well to say, that preliminary arrangements were made in a number of places—plans proposed, discussed and decided upon, numbers invited to participate in the movement, and the list of adherents increased.

Nine insurrections is the number given by some as the true list of outbreaks since slavery was planted in America; whether correct or not, it is certain that preliminaries to each are unquestionable. Gabriel, Vesey, Nat Turner, all had conference meetings; all had their plans; but they differ from the Harper's Ferry insurrection in the fact that neither leader nor men, in the latter, divulged ours, when in the most trying of situations.

Hark and another met Nat Turner in secret places, after the fatigues of a toilsome day were ended; Gabriel promulgated his treason in the silence of the dense forest; but John Brown reasoned of liberty and equality in broad daylight, in a modernized building, in conventions with closed doors, in meetings governed by the elaborate regulations laid down by Jefferson, and used as their guides by Congresses and Legislatures; or he made known the weighty theme, and his comprehensive plans resulting from it, by the cozy fireside, at familiar social gatherings of chosen ones, or better, in the carefully arranged junto of earnest, practical men.

Vague hints, careful blinds, are Nat Turner's entire make-up to save detection; the telegraph, the post-office, the railway, all were made to aid the new outbreak. By this, it will be seen that Insurrection has its progressive side, and has been elevated by John Brown from the skulking, fearing cabal, when in the hands of a brave but despairing few, to the highly organized, formidable, and to very many, indispensable institution for the security of freedom, when guided by intelligence.

So much as relates to prior movements may safely be said above; but who met—when they met—how many yet await the propitious moment—upon whom the mantle of John Brown has fallen to lead on the future army—the certain, terribly certain, many who must follow up the work, forgetting not to gather up the blood of the hero and his slain, to the humble bondman there offered—these may not, must not be told!

Of the many meetings in various places, before the work commenced, I shall speak just here of the one, the minutes of which were dragged forth by marauding Virginians from the "archives" at Kennedy Farm; not forgetting, however, for their comfort, that the Convention was one of a series at Chatham, some of which were of equally great, if not greater, importance.

The first visit of John Brown to Chatham was in April, 1858. Wherever he went around, although an entire stranger, he made a profound impression upon those who saw or became acquainted with him. Some supposed him to be a staid but modernized Quaker; others, a solid business man, from "somewhere," and without question a philanthropist.

His long white beard, thoughtful and reverent brow and physiognomy, his sturdy, measured tread, as he circulated about with hands, as portrayed in the best lithograph, under the pendant coat-skirt of plain brown Tweed, with other garments to match, revived to those honored with his acquaintance and knowing his history, the memory of a Puritan of the most exalted type.

After some important business, preparatory to the Convention, was finished, Mr. Brown went West, and returned with his men, who had been spending the winter in Iowa. The party, including the old gentleman, numbered twelve—as brave, intelligent and earnest a company as could have been associated in one party.

There were John H. Kagi, Aaron D. Stevens, Owen Brown, Richard Realf, George B. Gill, C.W. Moffitt, Wm. H. Leeman, John E. Cook, Stewart Taylor, Richard Richardson, Charles P. Tidd and J.S. Parsons—all white except Richard Richardson, who was a slave in Missouri until helped to his liberty by Captain Brown. At a meeting held to prepare for the Convention and to examine the Constitution, Dr. M.R. Delany was Chairman, and John H. Kagi and myself were the Secretaries.

When the Convention assembled, the minutes of which were seized by the slaveholding "cravens" at the Farm, and which, as they have been identified, I shall append to this chapter, Mr. Brown unfolded his plans and purpose.

He regarded slavery as a state of perpetual war against the slave, and was fully impressed with the idea that himself and his friends had the right to take liberty, and to use arms in defending the same. Being a devout Bible Christian, he sustained his views and shaped his plans in conformity to the Bible; and when setting them forth, he quoted freely from the Scripture to sustain his position.

He realized and enforced the doctrine of destroying the tree that bringeth forth corrupt fruit. Slavery was to him the corrupt tree, and the duty of every Christian man was to strike down slavery, and to commit its fragments to the flames. He was listened to with profound attention, his views were adopted, and the men whose names form a part of the minutes of that in many respects extraordinary meeting, aided yet further in completing the work.

Minutes of the Convention

CHATHAM (Canada West)
Saturday, May 8, 1858—10 A.M.

Convention met in pursuance to a call of John Brown and others, and was called to order by Mr. Jackson, on whose motion, Mr. William C. Munroe was chosen President; when, on motion of Mr. Brown, Mr. J. H. Kagi was elected Secretary.

On motion of Mr. Delany, Mr. Brown then proceeded to the object of the Convention at length, and then to explain general features of the plan of action in the execution of the project in view by the Convention. Mr. Delany and others spoke in favor of the project and the plan, and both were agreed to by general consent.

Mr. Brown then presented a plan of organization, entitled "Provisional Constitution and Ordinances for the People of the United States," and moved the reading of the same.

Mr. Kinnard objected to the reading until an oath of secrecy was taken by each member of the Convention; whereupon Mr. Delany moved that the following parole of honor be taken by all the members of the Convention— "I solemnly affirm that I will not in any way divulge any of the secrets of this Convention except to persons entitled to know the same, on the pain of forfeiting the respect and protection of this organization;" which motion was carried.

The President then proceeded to administer the obligation, after which the question was taken on the reading of the plan proposed by Mr. Brown, and the same carried.

The plan was then read by the Secretary, after which, on motion of Mr. Whipple, it was ordered that it be now read by articles for consideration.

The articles from one to forty-five, inclusive, were then read and adopted. On the reading of the forty-sixth, Mr. Reynolds moved to strike out the same. Reynolds spoke in favor, and Brown, Munroe, Owen Brown, Delany, Realf, Kinnard and Kagi against. The question was then taken and lost, there being but one vote in the affirmative. The article was then adopted.

The forty-seventh and forty-eighth articles, with the schedule, were then adopted in the same manner. It was then moved by Mr. Delany that the title and preamble stand as read. Carried.

On motion of Mr. Kagi, the Constitution, as a whole, was then unanimously adopted.

The Convention then, at half-past one o'clock, P.M., adjourned, on motion of Mr. Jackson, till three o'clock.

THREE O'CLOCK, P.M. Journal read and approved.

On motion of Mr. Delany, it was then ordered that those approving of the Constitution as adopted sign the same; whereupon the names of all the members were appended.

After congratulatory remarks by Messrs. Kinnard and Delany, the Convention, on motion of Mr. Whipple, adjourned at three and three-quarters o'clock.

J.H. KAGI, *Secretary of the Convention.*

The above is a journal of the Provisional Constitutional Convention held at Chatham, Canada West, May 8, 1858, as herein stated.

CHATHAM (Canada West), Saturday, May 8, 1858.

SIX P.M. In accordance with, and obedience to, the provisions of the schedule to the Constitution for the proscribed and oppressed people "of the United States of America," today adopted at this place, a Convention was called by the President of the Convention framing that instrument, and met at the above-named hour, for the purpose of electing officers to fill the offices specially established and named by said Constitution.

The Convention was called to order by Mr. M.R. Delany, upon whose nomination, Mr. Wm. C. Munroe was chosen President, and Mr. J.H. Kagi, Secretary.

A Committee, consisting of Messrs. Whipple, Kagi, Bell, Cook and Munroe, was then chosen to select candidates for the various offices to be filled, for the consideration of the Convention.

On reporting progress, and asking leave to sit again, the request was refused, and Committee discharged.

On motion of Mr. Bell, the Convention then went into the election of officers, in the following manner and order: —

Mr. Whipple nominated John Brown for Commander-in-Chief, who, on the seconding of Mr. Delany, was elected by acclamation.

Mr. Realf nominated J.H. Kagi for Secretary of War, who was elected in the same manner.

On motion of Mr. Brown, the Convention then adjourned to 9, AM., on Monday, the 10th.

MONDAY, May 10, 1858—NINE A.M. The Proceedings of the convention on Saturday were read and approved.

The President announced that the business before the Convention was the further election of officers.

Mr. Whipple nominated Thomas M. Kinnard for President. In a speech of some length, Mr Kinnard declined.

Mr. Anderson nominated J.W. Loguen for the same office. The nomination was afterwards withdrawn, Mr. Loguen not being present, and it being announced that he would not serve if elected.

Mr. Brown then moved to postpone the election of President for the present. Carried.

The Convention then went into the election of members of Congress. Messrs. A.M. Ellsworth and Osborne Anderson were elected.

After which, the Convention went into the election of Secretary of State, to which office Richard Realf was chosen.

Whereupon the Convention adjourned to half-past two, P.M.

2 1/4, P.M. Convention again assembled, and went into a balloting for the election of Treasurer and Secretary of the Treasury. Owen Brown was elected as the former, and George B. Gill as the latter.

The following resolution was then introduced by Mr. Brown, and unanimously passed: —

Resolved, That John Brown, J.H. Kagi, Richard Realf, L.F. Parsons, C.P. Todd, C. Whipple, C.W. Moffit, John E. Cook, Owen Brown, Stewart Taylor, Osborne Anderson, A.M. Ellsworth, Richard Richardson, W.H. Leeman and John Lawrence be and are hereby appointed a Committee to whom is delegated the power of the Convention to fill by election all the offices specially named in the Provisional Constitution which may be vacant after the adjournment of this Convention.

The Convention then adjourned, *sine die.*

J.H. KAGI, *Secretary of the Convention.*

Names of Members of the Convention, Written by Each Person

William Charles Munroe, President of the Convention; G.J. Reynolds, J.C. Grant, A.J. Smith, James M. Jones, George B. Gill, M.F. Bailey, William Lambert, S. Hunton, C.W. Moffit, John J. Jackson, J. Anderson, Alfred Whipple, James M. Buel, W.H. Leeman, Alfred M. Ellsworth, John E. Cook, Stewart Taylor, James W. Purnell, George Aiken, Stephen Dettin, Thomas Hickerson, John Caunel, Robinson Alexander, Richard Realf, Thomas F. Cary, Richard Richardson, L.F. Parsons, Thomas M. Kinnard, M.H. Delany, Robert Vanvanken, Thomas M. Stringer, Charles P. Tidd, John A. Thomas, C. Whipple, I.D. Shadd, Robert Newman, Owen Brown, John Brown, J.H. Harris, Charles Smith, Simon Fislin, Isaac Holler, James Smith, J.H. Kagi, Secretary of the Convention.

CHAPTER III

Many affect to despise the Chatham Convention, and the persons who there abetted the "treason." Governor Wise would like nothing better than to engage the Canadas, with but ten men under his command. By that it is clear that the men acquainted with Brown's plans would not be a "breakfast-spell" for the chivalrous Virginian.

In one respect, they were not formidable, and their Constitution would seem to be a harmless paper. Some of them were outlaws against Buchanan Democratic rule in the Territories; some were colored men who had felt severely the proscriptive spirit of American caste; others were escaped slaves, who had left dear kindred behind, writhing in the bloody grasp of the vile man-stealer, never, never to be released, until some practical, daring, determined step should be taken by their friends or their escaped brethren.

What use could such men make of a Constitution? Destitute of political or social power, as respects the American States and people, what ghost of an echo could they invoke, by declamation or action, against the peculiar institution?

In the light of slaveholding logic and its conclusions, they were but renegade whites and insolent blacks; but, aggregating their grievances, summing up their deep-seated hostility to a system to which every precept of morality, every tie of relationship, is a perpetual protest, the men in Convention, and the many who could not conveniently attend at the time, were not a handful to be despised. The braggadocio of the Virginia Governor might be eager to engage them with ten slaveholders, but John Brown was satisfied with them, and that is honor enough for a generation.

After the Convention adjourned, other business was despatched with utmost speed, and everyone seemed in good spirits. The "boys" of the party of "Surveyors," as they were called, were the admired of those who knew them, and the subject of curious remark and inquiry by strangers. So many intellectual looking men are seldom seen in one party, and at the same time, such utter disregard of prevailing custom, or style, in dress and other little conventionalities.

Hour after hour they would sit in council, thoughtful, ready; some of them eloquent, all fearless, patient of the fatigues of business; anon, here and there over the "track," and again in the assembly; when the time for relaxation came, sallying forth arm in arm, un-shaven, unshorn, and altogether indifferent about it; or one, it may be, impressed with the coming responsibility, sauntering alone, in earnest thought, apparently indifferent to all outward objects, but ready at a word or sign from the chief to undertake any task.

During the sojourn at Chatham, the commissions to the men were discussed, &c. It has been a matter of inquiry, even among friends, why colored men were not commissioned by John Brown to act as captains, lieutenants, &c. I reply, with the knowledge that men in the movement now living will confirm it, that John Brown did offer the captaincy, and other military positions, to colored men equally with others, but a want of acquaintance with military tactics was the in-variable excuse.

Holding a civil position, as we termed it, I declined a captain's commission tendered by the brave old man, as better suited to those more experienced; and as I was willing to give my life to the cause, trusting to experience and fidelity to make me more worthy, my ex-cuse was accepted. The same must be said of other colored men to be spoken of hereafter, and who proved their worthiness by their able defence of freedom at the Ferry.

John H. Kagi

Of the constellation of noble men who came to Chatham with Captain Brown, no one was greater in the essentials of true nobility of character and executive skill than John H. Kagi, the confidential friend and adviser of the old man, and second in position in the expedition; no one was held in more deserved respect. Kagi was, singularly enough, a Virginian by birth, and had relatives in the region of the Ferry. He left home when a youth, an enemy to slavery, and brought as his gift offering to freedom three slaves, whom he piloted to the North. His innate hatred of the institution made him a willing exile from the State of his birth, and his great abilities, natural and acquired, entitled him to the position he held in Captain Brown's confidence.

Kagi was indifferent to personal appearance; he often went about with slouched hat, one leg of his pantaloons properly adjusted, and the other partly tucked into his high boot-top; unbrushed, unshaven, and in utter disregard of "the latest style"; but to his companions and acquaintances, a verification of Burns' man in the clothes; for John Henry Kagi had improved his time; he discoursed elegantly and fluently, wrote ably, and could occupy the platform with greater ability than many a man known to the American people as famous in these respects. John Brown appreciated him, and to his men, his estimate of John Henry was a familiar theme.

Kagi's bravery, his devotion to the cause, his deference to the commands of his leader, were most nobly illustrated in his conduct at Harper's Ferry.

Scarcely had the Convention and other meetings and business at Chatham been concluded, and most necessary work been done, both at St. Catherines and at this point, when the startling intelligence that the plans were exposed came to hand, and that "Judas" Forbes, after having disclosed some of our important arrangements in the Middle States, was on his way to Washington on a similar errand.

This news caused an entire change in the programme for a time. The old gentleman went one way, the young men another, but ultimately to meet in Kansas, in part, where the summer was spent.

In the winter of that year, Captain Brown, J.H. Kagi, A.D. Stevens, C.P. Tidd and Owen Brown, went into Missouri, and released a company of slaves, whom they eventually escorted to Canada, where they are now living and taking care of themselves. An incident of that slave rescue may serve to illustrate more fully the spirit pervading the old man and his "boys." After leaving Missouri with the fugitives, and while yet pursuing the perilous hegira, birth was given to a male child by one of the slave mothers. Dr. Doy, of Kansas, aided in the accouchement, and walked five miles afterwards to get new milk for the boy, while the old Captain named him John Brown, after himself, which name he now bears.

At that time, a reward from the United States government was upon the head of Brown; United States Marshals were whisking about, pretendedly eager to arrest them; the weather was very cold, and dangers were upon every hand; but not one jot of comfort or attention for the tender babe and its invalid mother was abated. No thought for their valuable selves, but only how best might the poor and despised charge in their keeping be prudently but really nursed and guarded in their trial journey for liberty. Noble leader of a noble company of men!

Yes, reader, whether at Harper's Ferry, or paving the way thither with such deeds as the one here told, and well known West, the old hero and that company were philanthropists to the core. I do not know if the wicked scheme of Forbes may not be excused a little, solely because it afforded the occasion for the great enterprise, growing out of this last visit to Kansas; but Forbes himself must nevertheless be held guilty for its inception, as only ambition to usurp power, and his great love of self (peculiar to him, of all connected with Captain Brown) made him dissatisfied, and determined to add falsehood to his other sins against John Brown.

"Judas" Forbes

This Forbes, who, though pretending to disclose some dangerous hornet's nest, was careful enough of his worthless self to tell next to nothing, but to resort to lies, rather from a clear understanding of the consequences, if caught, is an Englishman.

When information came, it was not known how much he had told or how little; therefore Brown's precaution to proceed West. From the spring of '58 to the autumn of '59, getting no intelligence of him, it was said he had left America; but instead of that, he lurked around in disguise, feeling, no doubt, that he deserved the punishment of death.

Before his defection, he entered into agreement with Captain Brown to work in the cause of emancipation upon the same terms as did the others, as I repeatedly learned from Brown and his associates, who were acquainted with the matter, and whose veracity stands infinitely above Forbes' word. From Brown, Kagi and Stevens, I learned that the position of second in the organization under the Captain was to be held by "Judas," because of his acquaintance with military science. He was to be drill-master of the company, but not to receive one particle of salary more than the youngest man in the company.

But having once gained a secure foothold, he sought to carry out his evil design to make money out of philanthropy, or destroy the movement forever, could he not be well paid to remain quiet. Money was his object from the first, though disguised; and when he failed to secure that, he raised the question of leadership with Captain Brown, and that was his excuse for withdrawing from the movement. His heart was clearly never right; but he only delayed, he did not stop the work.

When the outbreak occurred, he figured for a little while, though very cautiously, and finally fled to Europe, another Cain, whose mark is unmistakable, and who had better never been born than attempt to stand up among the men he so greatly wronged.

CHAPTER IV

Throughout the Summer of 1859, when everything wore the appearance of perfect quiet, when suspicions were all lulled, when those not fully initiated thought the whole scheme was abandoned, arrangements were in active preparation for the work. Mr. Brown, Kagi, and a part of the Harper's Ferry company, who had previously spent some time in Ohio, went into Pennsylvania in the month of June, and up to the early part of July, having made necessary observations, they penetrated the Keystone yet further, and laid plans to receive freight and men as they should arrive. Under the assumed name of Smith, Captain Brown pushed his explorations further south, and selected:

Kennedy Farm

Kennedy Farm, in every respect an excellent location for *business* as "headquarters," was rented at a cheap rate, and men and freight were sent thither. Captain Brown returned to —, and sent freight, while Kagi was stationed at —, to correspond with persons elsewhere, and to receive and dispatch freight as it came. Owen, Watson, and Oliver Brown, took their position at headquarters, to receive whatever was sent. These completed the arrangements.

The Captain labored and traveled night and day, sometimes on old Dolly, his brown mule, and sometimes in the wagon. He would start directly after night, and travel the fifty miles between the Farm and Chambersburg by daylight next morning; and he otherwise kept open communication between headquarters and the latter place, in order that matters might be arranged in due season.

John H. Kagi wrote for freight, and the following letter, before published in relation to it, was written by a co-laborer:

WEST ANDOVER, Ohio, July 30th, 1859
JOHN HENRIE, Esq.:

DEAR SIR, —I yesterday received yours of the 25th inst., together with letter of instructions from our mutual friend Isaac, enclosing draft for $100. Have written you as many as three letters, I think, before this, and have received all you have sent, probably.

The heavy freight of fifteen boxes I sent off some days ago. The household stuff, consisting of six boxes and one chest, I have put in good shape, and shall, I think, be able to get them on their way on Monday next, and shall myself be on my way northward within a day or two after.

Enclosed please find list of contents of boxes, which it may be well to preserve.

The freight having arrived in good condition, John Henrie replies.

As the Kennedy Farm is a part of history, a slight allusion to its location may not be out of place, although it has been so frequently spoken of as to be almost universally known.

The Farm is located in Washington County, Maryland, in a mountainous region, on the road from Chambersburg; it is in a comparatively non-slaveholding population, four miles from Harper's Ferry. Yet, among the few traders in the souls of men located around, several circumstances peculiar to the institution happened while the party sojourned there, which serve to show up its hideous character.

During three weeks of my residence at the Farm, no less than four deaths took place among the slaves; one, Jerry, living three miles away, hung himself in the late Dr. Kennedy's orchard, because he was to be sold South, his master having become insolvent. The other three cases were homicides; they were punished so that death ensued immediately, or in a short time.

It was the knowledge of these atrocities, and the melancholy suicide named, that caused Oliver Brown, when writing to his young wife, to refer directly to the deplorable aspect of slavery in that neighborhood. Once fairly established, and freight having arrived safely, the published correspondence becomes significant to an actor in the scene. Emigrants began to drop down, from this quarter and the other. Smith writes to Kagi:

WEST ANDOVER, Ashtabula Co., Wednesday, 1859.
FRIEND HENRIE,

—Yours of the 14th inst. I received last night—glad to learn that the "Wire" has arrived in good condition, and that our "R" friend was pleased with a view of those "pre-eventful shadows."

Shall write Leary at once, also our other friends at the North and East. Am highly pleased with the prospect I have of doing something to the purpose now, right away, here and in contiguous sections, in the way of getting stock taken. I am devoting my whole time to our work. Write often, and keep me posted up close. (Here follow some phonographic characters, which may be read: "I have learned phonography, but not enough to correspond to any advantage. Can probably read anything you may write, if written in the corresponding style.")

Faithfully yours, JOHN SMITH.

Please say to father to address (phonographic characters which might read "John Luther") when he writes me. I wish you to see what I have written him.

J.S.

The Agent

In the month of August, 1859, John Brown's Agent spent some time in Canada. He visited Chatham, Buxton, and other places, and formed Liberty Leagues, and arranged matters so that operations could be carried on with excellent success, through the efficiency of Messrs. C., S., B., and L., the Chairman, Corresponding Secretary, Secretary O., and Treasurer of the Society. He then proceeded to Detroit, where another Society is established.

So well satisfied was Captain Brown with the work done, that he wrote in different directions: "The fields whiten unto harvest;" and again, "Your friends at headquarters want you at their elbow." This was an invitation by the good old man to be as brave and efficient a laborer in the cause of human rights as the friends of freedom have ever known; and to one who must bear the beacon-light of liberty before the self-emancipated bondsmen of the South.

CHAPTER V

More Correspondence—My Journey to the Ferry—A Glance at the Family

Preparations had so far progressed, up to the time when incidents mentioned in the preceding chapter had taken place, that Kagi wrote to Chatham and other places, urging parties favorable to come on without loss of time. In reply to the letter written to Chatham, soliciting volunteers, the appended, from an office-bearer, referred to my own journey to the South:

DEAR SIR,

Yours came to hand last night. One hand (Anderson) left here last night, and will be found an efficient hand. Richardson is anxious to be at work as a missionary to bring sinners to repentance. He will start in a few days. Another will follow immediately after, if not with him. More laborers may be looked for shortly. "Slow but sure."

Alexander has received yours, so you see all communications have come to hand, so far. Alexander is not coming up to the work as he agreed. I fear he will be found unreliable in the end.

Dull times affect missionary matters here more than any thing else; however, a few active laborers may be looked for as certain.

I would like to hear of your congregation numbering more than "15 and 2" to commence a good revival; still, our few will be adding strength to the good work.

Yours, & C.,   J.M.B.
To J.B. Jr.

As set forth in this letter, I left Canada September 13th, and reached ——, in Pennsylvania, three days after. On my arrival, I was surprised to learn that the freight was all moved to headquarters, but a few boxes, the arrival of which, the evening of the same day, called forth from Kagi the following brief note:

CHAMBERSBURG, ——, ——.

J. SMITH & SONS,

A quantity of freight has today arrived for you in care of Oaks & Caufman. The amount is somewhere between 2,600 and 3,000 lbs. Charges in full, $25.98. The character is, according to manifest, 33 bundles and 4 boxes.

I yesterday received a letter from John Smith, containing nothing of any particular importance, however, so I will keep it until you come up.

Respectfully,   J. HENRIE.

CHAMBERSBURG, Pa.,
Friday, Sept. 16, 1859, 11 o'clock, A.M.

J. SMITH AND SONS,

I have just time to say that Mr. Anderson arrived in the train five minutes ago.

Respectfully,   J. HENRIE.

P. S. I have not had time to talk with him.   J. H.

A little while prior to this, * * went down to ——, to accompany Shields Green, whereupon a meeting of Captain Brown, Kagi, and other distinguished persons, convened for consultation.

On the 20th, four days after I reached this outpost, Captain Brown, Watson Brown, Kagi, myself, and several friends, held another meeting, after which, on the 24th, I left Chambersburg for Kennedy Farm. I walked alone as far as Middletown, a town on the line between Maryland and Pennsylvania, and it being dark, I found Captain Brown awaiting with his wagon.

We set out directly, and drove until nearly daybreak the next morning, when we reached the Farm in safety. As a very necessary precaution against surprise, all the colored men at the Ferry who went from the North, made the journey from the Pennsylvania line in the night.

I found all the men concerned in the undertaking on hand when I arrived, excepting Copeland, Leary, and Merriam; and when all had collected, a more earnest, fearless, determined company of men it would be difficult to get together. There, as at Chatham, I saw the same evidence of strong and commanding intellect, high-toned morality, and inflexibility of purpose in the men, and a profound and holy reverence for God, united to the most comprehensive, practical, systematic philanthropy, and undoubted bravery in the patriarch leader, brought out to view in lofty grandeur by the associations and surroundings of the place and the occasion.

There was no milk and water sentimentality—no offensive contempt for the negro, while working in his cause; the pulsations of each and every heart beat in harmony for the suffering and pleading slave. I thank God that I have been permitted to realize to its furthest, fullest extent, the moral, mental, physical, social harmony of an Anti-Slavery family, carrying out to the letter the principles of its ante-type, the Anti-Slavery cause. In John Brown's house, and in John Brown's presence, men from widely different parts of the continent met and united into one company, wherein no hateful prejudice dared intrude its ugly self—no ghost of a distinction found space to enter.

CHAPTER VI

Life at Kennedy Farm

To a passer-by, the house and its surroundings presented but indifferent attractions. Any log tenement of equal dimensions would be as likely to arrest a stray glance. Rough, unsightly, and aged, it was only those privileged to enter and tarry for a long time, and to penetrate the mysteries of the two rooms it contained—kitchen, parlor, dining-room below, and the spacious chamber, attic, store-room, prison, drilling room, comprised in the loft above—who could tell how we lived at Kennedy Farm.

Every morning, when the noble old man was at home, he called the family around, read from his Bible, and offered to God most fervent and touching supplications for all flesh; and especially pathetic were his petitions in behalf of the oppressed. I never heard John Brown pray, that he did not make strong appeals to God for the deliverance of the slave.

This duty over, the men went to the loft, there to remain all the day long; few only could be seen about, as the neighbors were watchful and suspicious. It was also important to talk but little among ourselves, as visitors to the house might be curious. Besides the daughter and the daughter-in-law, who superintended the work, some one or other of the men was regularly detailed to assist in the cooking, washing, and other domestic work. After the ladies left, we did all the work, no one being exempt, because of age or official grade in the organization.

The principal employment of the prisoners, as we severally were when compelled to stay in the loft, was to study Forbes' Manual, and to go through a quiet, though rigid drill, under the training of Captain Stevens, at some times. At others, we applied a preparation for bronzing our gun barrels—discussed subjects of reform—related our personal history; but when our resources became pretty well exhausted, the *ennui* from confinement, imposed silence, etc., would make the men almost desperate. At such times, neither slavery nor slaveholders were discussed mincingly.

We were, while the ladies remained, often relieved of much of the dullness growing out of restraint by their kindness. As we could not circulate freely, they would bring in wild fruit and flowers from the woods and fields. We were well supplied with grapes, paw-paws, chestnuts, and other small fruit, besides bouquets of fall flowers, through their thoughtful consideration.

During the several weeks I remained at the encampment, we were under the restraint I write of through the day; but at night, we sallied out for a ramble, or to breathe the fresh air and enjoy the beautiful solitude of the mountain scenery around, by moonlight.

Captain Brown loved the fullest expression of opinion from his men, and not seldom, when a subject was being severely scrutinized by Kagi, Oliver, or others of the party, the old gentleman would be one of the most interested and earnest hearers. Frequently his views were severely criticised, when no one would be in better spirits than himself. He often remarked that it was gratifying to see young men grapple with moral and other important questions, and express themselves independently; it was evidence of self-sustaining power.

CHAPTER VII

Being obliged, from the space I propose to give to this narrative, to omit many incidents of my sojourn at the Farm, which from association are among my most pleasant recollections, the events now to be recorded are to me invested with the most intense interest.

About ten days before the capture of the Ferry, Captain John Brown and Kagi went to Philadelphia, on business of great importance. How important, men there and elsewhere *now* know. How affected by, and affecting the main features of the enterprise, we at the Farm knew full well after their return, as the old Captain, in the fullness of his overflowing, saddened heart, detailed point after point of interest. God bless the old veteran, who could and did chase a thousand in life, and defied more than ten thousand by the moral sublimity of his death!

On their way home, at Chambersburg, they met young F.J. Merriam of Boston. Several days were spent at C., when Merriam left for Baltimore, to purchase some necessary articles for the undertaking. John Copeland and Sherrard Lewis Leary reached Chambersburg on the 12th of October, and on Saturday, the 15th, at daylight, they arrived, in company with Kagi and Watson Brown. In the evening of the same day, F. J. Merriam came to the Farm.

Saturday, the 15th, was a busy day for all hands. The chief and every man worked busily, packing up, and getting ready to remove the means of defence to the schoolhouse, and for further security, as the people living around were in a state of excitement, from having seen a number of men about the premises a few days previously.

Not being fully satisfied as to the real business of "J. Smith & Sons" after that, and learning that several thousand stand of arms were to be removed by the Government from the Armory to some other point, threats to search the premises were made against the encampment.

A tried friend having given information of the state of public feeling without, and of the intended process, Captain Brown and party concluded to strike a blow immediately, and not, as at first intended, to await certain reinforcements from the North and East, which would have been in Maryland within one and three weeks.

Could other parties, waiting for the word, have reached headquarters in time for the outbreak when it took place, the taking of the armory, engine house, and rifle factory, would have been quite different. But the men at the Farm had been so closely confined, that they went out about the house and farm in the daytime during that week, and so indiscreetly exposed their numbers to the prying neighbors, who thereupon took steps to have a search instituted in the early part of the coming week.

Captain Brown was not seconded in another quarter as he expected at the time of the action, but could the fears of the neighbors have been allayed for a few days, the disappointment in the former respect would not have had much weight.

The indiscretion alluded to has been greatly lamented by all of us, as Maryland, Virginia, and other slave States, had, as they now have, a direct interest in the successful issue of the first step. Few ultimately successful movements were predicated on the issue of the first bold stroke, and so it is with the institution of slavery. It will yet come down by the run, but it will not be because huzzas of victory were shouted over the first attempt, any more than at Bunker Hill or Hastings.

CHAPTER VIII

On Sunday morning, October 16th, Captain Brown arose earlier than usual, and called his men down to worship. He read a chapter from the Bible, applicable to the condition of the slaves, and our duty as their brethren, and then offered up a fervent prayer to God to assist in the liberation of the bondmen in that slaveholding land. The services were impressive beyond expression. Every man there assembled seemed to respond from the depths of his soul, and throughout the entire day, a deep solemnity pervaded the place. The old man's usually weighty words were invested with more than ordinary importance, and the countenance of every man reflected the momentous thought that absorbed his attention within.

After breakfast had been despatched, and the roll called by the Captain, a sentinel was posted outside the door, to warn by signal if any one should approach, and we listened to preparatory remarks to a council meeting to be held that day.

At 10 o'clock, the council was assembled. I was appointed to the Chair, when matters of importance were considered at length. After the council adjourned, the Constitution was read for the benefit of the few who had not before heard it, and the necessary oaths taken. Men who were to hold military positions in the organization, and who had not received commissions before then, had their commissions filled out by J.H. Kagi, and gave the required obligations.

In the afternoon, the eleven orders presented in the next chapter were given by the Captain, and were afterwards carried out in every particular by the officers and men.

In the evening, before setting out to the Ferry, he gave his final charge, in which he said, among other things:—*"And now, gentlemen, let me impress this one thing upon your minds. You all know how dear life is to you, and how dear your life is to your friends. And in remembering that, consider that the lives of others are as dear to them as yours are to you. Do not, therefore, take the life of any one, if you can possibly avoid it; but if it is necessary to take life in order to save your own, then make sure work of it."*

CHAPTER IX

The Eleven Orders Given by Captain Brown to His Men before Setting out for the Ferry

The orders given by Captain Brown, before departing from the Farm for the Ferry, were: —

1. Captain Owen Brown, F.J. Merriam, and Barclay Coppic to remain at the old house as sentinels, to guard the arms and effects till morning, when they would be joined by some of the men from the Ferry with teams to move all arms and other things to the old school-house before referred to, located about three-quarters of a mile from Harper's Ferry—a place selected a day or two beforehand by the Captain.

2. All hands to make as little noise as possible going to the Ferry, so as not to attract attention till we could get to the bridge; and to keep all arms secreted, so as not to be detected if met by any one.

3. The men were to walk in couples, at some distance apart; and should any one overtake us, stop him and detain him until the rest of our comrades were out of the road. The same course to be pursued if we were met by any one.

4. That Captains Charles P. Tidd and John E. Cook walk ahead of the wagon in which Captain Brown rode to the Ferry, to tear down the telegraph wires on the Maryland side along the railroad; and to do the same on the Virginia side, after the town should be captured.

5. Captains John H. Kagi and A.D. Stevens were to take the watchman at the Ferry bridge prisoner when the party got there, and to detain him here until the engine house upon the Government grounds should be taken.

6. Captain Watson Brown and Stewart Taylor were to take positions at the Potomac bridge and hold it till morning. They were to stand on opposite sides, a rod apart, and if any one entered the

bridge, they were to let him get in between them. In that case, pikes were to be used, not Sharp's rifles, unless they offered much resistance, and refused to surrender.

7. Captains Oliver Brown and William Thompson were to execute a similar order at Shenandoah bridge, until morning.

8. Lieutenant Jeremiah Anderson and Adolphus Thompson were to occupy the engine house at first, with the prisoner watchman from the bridge and the watchman belonging to the engine-house yard, until the one on the opposite side of the street and the rifle factory were taken, after which they would be reinforced, to hold that place with the prisoners.

9. Lieutenant Albert Hazlett and Private Edwin Coppic were to hold the Armory opposite the engine house after it had been taken, through the night and until morning, when arrangements would be different.

10. That John H. Kagi, Adjutant General, and John A. Copeland (colored) take positions at the rifle factory through the night, and hold it until further orders.

11. That Colonel A.D. Stevens (the same Captain Stevens who held military position next to Captain Brown) proceed to the country with his men, and after taking certain parties prisoners bring them to the Ferry. In the case of Colonel Lewis Washington, who had arms in his hands, he must, before being secured as a prisoner, deliver them into the hands of Osborne P. Anderson. Anderson being a colored man, and colored men being only things in the South, it is proper that the South be taught a lesson upon this point.

John H. Kagi being Adjutant General, was the near adviser of Captain John Brown, and second in position; and had the old gentleman been slain at the Ferry, and Kagi been spared, the command would have devolved upon the latter. But Colonel Stevens holding the active military position in the organization second to Captain Brown, when order eleven was given him, had the privilege of choosing his own men to execute it.

The selection was made after the capture of the Ferry, and then my duty to receive Colonel Washington's famous arms was assigned me by Captain Brown. The men selected by Colonel Stevens to act under his orders during the night were Charles P. Tidd, Osborne P. Anderson, Shields Green, John E. Cook, and Sherrard Lewis Leary. We were to take prisoners, and any slaves who would come, and bring them to the Ferry.

A few days before, Captain Cook had traveled along the Charlestown turnpike, and collected statistics of the population of slaves and the masters' names. Among the masters whose acquaintance Cook had made, Colonel Washington had received him politely, and had shown him a sword formerly owned by Frederic the Great of Prussia, and presented by him to General Washington, and a pair of horse pistols, formerly owned by General Lafayette, and bequeathed by the old General to Lewis Washington. These were the arms specially referred to in the charge.

At eight o'clock on Sunday evening, Captain Brown said: "Men, get on your arms; we will proceed to the Ferry." His horse and wagon were brought out before the door, and some pikes, a sledge-hammer and crowbar were placed in it.

The Captain then put on his old Kansas cap, and said: "Come, boys!" when we marched out of the camp behind him, into the lane leading down the hill to the main road.

As we formed the procession line, Owen Brown, Barclay Coppic, and Francis J. Merriam, sentinels left behind to protect the place as before stated, came forward and took leave of us; after which, agreeably to previous orders, and as they were better acquainted with the topography of the Ferry, and to effect the tearing down of the telegraph wires, C.P. Tidd and John E. Cook led the procession.

While going to the Ferry, the company marched along as solemnly as a funeral procession, till we got to the bridge. When we entered, we halted, and carried out an order to fasten our cartridge boxes outside of our clothes, when everything was ready for taking the town.

CHAPTER X

The Capture of Harper's Ferry—Col. A.D. Stevens and Party Sally out to the Plantations—What We Saw, Heard, Did, Etc.

As John H. Kagi and A.D. Stevens entered the bridge, as ordered in the fifth charge, the watchman, being at the other end, came toward them with a lantern in his hand. When up to them, they told him he was their prisoner, and detained him a few minutes, when he asked them to spare his life. They replied, they did not intend to harm him; the object was to free the slaves, and he would have to submit to them for a time, in order that the purpose might be carried out.

Captain Brown now entered the bridge in his wagon, followed by the rest of us, until we reached that part where Kagi and Stevens held their prisoner, when he ordered Watson Brown and Stewart Taylor to take the positions assigned them in order sixth, and the rest of us to proceed to the engine house.

We started for the engine house, taking the prisoner along with us. When we neared the gates of the engine-house yard, we found them locked, and the watchman on the inside. He was told to open the gates, but refused, and commenced to cry. The men were then ordered by Captain Brown to open the gates forcibly, which was done, and the watchman taken prisoner.

The two prisoners were left in the custody of Jerry Anderson and Adolphus Thompson, and A.D. Stevens arranged the men to take possession of the Armory and rifle factory. About this time, there was apparently much excitement. People were passing back and forth in the town, and before we could do much, we had to take several prisoners. After the prisoners were secured, we passed to the opposite side of the street and took the Armory, and Albert Hazlett and Edwin Coppic were ordered to hold it for the time being.

The capture of the rifle factory was the next work to be done. When we went there, we told the watchman who was outside of the building our business, and asked him to go along with us, as we had come to take possession of the town, and make use of the Armory in carrying out our object. He obeyed the command without hesitation. John H. Kagi and John Copeland were placed in the Armory, and the prisoners taken to the engine house.

Following the capture of the Armory, Oliver Brown and William Thompson were ordered to take possession of the bridge leading out of town, across the Shenandoah river, which they immediately did. These places were all taken, and the prisoners secured, without the snap of a gun, or any violence whatever.

The town being taken, Brown, Stevens, and the men who had no post in charge, returned to the engine house, where council was held, after which Captain Stevens, Tidd, Cook, Shields Green, Leary and myself went to the country.

On the road, we met some colored men, to whom we made known our purpose, when they immediately agreed to join us. They said they had been long waiting for an opportunity of the kind. Stevens then asked them to go around among the colored people and circulate the news, when each started off in a different direction. The result was that many colored men gathered to the scene of action.

The first prisoner taken by us was Colonel Lewis Washington. When we neared his house, Captain Stevens placed Leary and Shields Green to guard the approaches to the house, the one at the side, the other in front. We then knocked, but no one answering, although females were looking from upper windows, we entered the building and commenced a search for the proprietor.

Colonel Washington opened his room door, and begged us not to kill him. Captain Stevens replied, "You are our prisoner," when he stood as if speechless or petrified. Stevens further told him to get ready to go the Ferry; that he had come to abolish slavery, not to take life but in self-defence, but that he must go along.

The Colonel replied: "You can have my slaves, if you will let me remain."

"No," said the Captain, "you must go along too; so get ready."

After saying this, Stevens left the house for a time, and with Green, Leary and Tidd, proceeded to the "Quarters," giving the prisoner in charge of Cook and myself. The male slaves were gathered together in a short time, when horses were tackled to the Colonel's two-horse carriage and four-horse wagon, and both vehicles brought to the front of the house.

During this time, Washington was walking the floor, apparently much excited. When the Captain came in, he went to the sideboard, took out his whiskey, and offered us something to drink, but he was refused. His fire-arms were next demanded, when he brought forth one double-barreled gun, one small rifle, two horse-pistols and a sword. Nothing else was asked of him.

The Colonel cried heartily when he found he must submit, and appeared taken aback when, on delivering up the famous sword formerly presented by Frederic to his illustrious kinsman George Washington, Captain Stevens told me to step forward and take it.

Washington was secured and placed in his wagon, the women of the family making great outcries, when the party drove forward to Mr. John Allstadt's. After making known our business to him, he went into as great a fever of excitement as Washington had done. We could have his slaves, also, if we would only leave him.

This, of course, was contrary to our plans and instructions. He hesitated, puttered around, fumbled and meditated for a long time. At last, seeing no alternative, he got ready, when the slaves were gathered up from about the quarters by their own consent, and all placed in Washington's big wagon and returned to the Ferry.

One old colored lady, at whose house we stopped, a little way from the town, had a good time over the message we took her. This liberating the slaves was the very thing she had longed for, prayed for, and dreamed about, time and again; and her heart was full of rejoicing over the fulfillment of a prophecy which had been her faith for long years.

While we were absent from the Ferry, the train of cars for Baltimore arrived, and was detained. A colored man named Haywood, employed upon it, went from the Wager House up to the entrance to the bridge, where the train stood, to assist with the baggage. He was ordered to stop by the sentinels stationed at the bridge, which he refused to do, but turned to go in an opposite direction, when he was fired upon, and received a mortal wound. Had he stood when ordered, he would not have been harmed. No one knew at the time whether he was white or colored, but his movements were such as to justify the sentinels in shooting him, as he would not stop when commanded.

The first firing happened at that time, and the only firing, until after daylight on Monday morning.

CHAPTER XI

Monday, the 17th of October, was a time of stirring and exciting events. In consequence of the movements of the night before, we were prepared for commotion and tumult, but certainly not for more than we beheld around us. Gray dawn and yet brighter daylight revealed great confusion, and as the sun arose, the panic spread like wild-fire.

Men, women and children could be seen leaving their homes in every direction; some seeking refuge among residents, and in quarters further away, others climbing up the hillsides, and hurrying off in various directions, evidently impelled by a sudden fear, which was plainly visible in their countenances or in their movements.

Captain Brown was all activity, though I could not help thinking that at times he appeared somewhat puzzled. He ordered Sherrard Lewis Leary, and four slaves, and a free man belonging in the neighborhood, to join John Henry Kagi and John Copeland at the rifle factory, which they immediately did.

Kagi, and all except Copeland, were subsequently killed, but not before having communicated with Captain Brown, as will be set forth further along.

As fast as the workmen came to the building, or persons appeared in the street near the engine house, they were taken prisoners, and directly after sunrise, the detained train was permitted to start for the eastward. After the departure of the train, quietness prevailed for a short time; a number of prisoners were already in the engine house, and of the many colored men living in the neighborhood, who had assembled in the town, a number were armed for the work.

Captain Brown ordered Captains Charles P. Tidd, Wm. H. Leeman, John E. Cook, and some fourteen slaves, to take Washington's four-horse wagon, and to join the company under Captain Owen Brown, consisting of F.J. Merriam and Barclay Coppic, who had been left at the Farm the night previous, to guard the place and the arms. The company, thus reinforced, proceeded, under Owen Brown, to move the arms and goods from the Farm down to the schoolhouse in the mountains, three-fourths of a mile from the Ferry.

Captain Brown next ordered me to take the pikes out of the wagon in which he rode to the Ferry, and to place them in the hands of the colored men who had come with us from the plantations, and others who had come forward without having had communication with any of our party.

It was out of the circumstances connected with the fulfillment of this order, that the false charge against "Anderson" as leader, or "ringleader," of the negroes, grew.

The spectators, about this time, became apparently wild with fright and excitement. The number of prisoners was magnified to hundreds, and the judgment-day could not have presented more terrors, in its awful and certain prospective punishment to the justly condemned for the wicked deeds of a life-time, the chief of which would no doubt be slaveholding, than did Captain Brown's operations.

The prisoners were also terror-stricken. Some wanted to go home to see their families, as if for the last time. The privilege was granted them, under escort, and they were brought back again. Edwin Coppic, one of the sentinels at the Armory gate, was fired at by one of the citizens, but the ball did not reach him, when one of the insurgents close by put up his rifle, and made the enemy bite the dust.

Among the arms taken from Colonel Washington was one double-barrel gun. This weapon was loaded by Leeman with buckshot, and placed in the hands of an elderly slave man, early in the morning. After the cowardly charge upon Coppic, this old man was ordered by Captain Stevens to arrest a citizen. The old man ordered him to halt, which he refused to do, when instantly the terrible load was discharged into him, and he fell, and expired without a struggle.

After these incidents, time passed away till the arrival of the United States troops, without any further attack upon us. The cowardly Virginians submitted like sheep, without resistance, from that time until the marines came down.

Meanwhile, Captain Brown, who was considering a proposition for release from his prisoners, passed back and forth from the Armory to the bridge, speaking words of comfort and encouragement to his men. "Hold on a little longer, boys," said he, "until I get matters arranged with the prisoners."

This tardiness on the part of our brave leader was sensibly felt to be an omen of evil by some of us, and was eventually the cause of our defeat. It was no part of the original plan to hold on to the Ferry, or to parley with prisoners; but by so doing, time was afforded to carry the news of its capture to several points, and forces were thrown into the place, which surrounded us.

At eleven o'clock, Captain Brown despatched William Thompson from the Ferry up to Kennedy Farm, with the news that we had peaceful possession of the town, and with directions to the men to continue on moving the things. He went; but before he could get back, troops had begun to pour in, and the general encounter commenced.

CHAPTER XII

Reception to the Troops—They Retreat to the Bridge—A Prisoner—Death of Dangerfield Newby—William Thompson—The Mountains Alive—Flag of Truce—The Engine House Taken

It was about twelve o'clock in the day when we were first attacked by the troops. Prior to that, Captain Brown, in anticipation of further trouble, had girded to his side the famous sword taken from Colonel Lewis Washington the night before, and with that memorable weapon, he commanded his men against General Washington's own State.

When the Captain received the news that the troops had entered the bridge from the Maryland side, he, with some of his men, went into the street, and sent a message to the Arsenal for us to come forth also.

We hastened to the street as ordered, when he said, "The troops are on the bridge, coming into town; we will give them a warm reception."

He then walked around amongst us, giving us words of encouragement, in this wise: "Men! Be cool! Don't waste your powder and shot! Take aim, and make every shot count!" "The troops will look for us to retreat on their first appearance; be careful to shoot first." Our men were well supplied with firearms, but Captain Brown had no rifle at that time; his only weapon was the sword before mentioned.

The troops soon came out of the bridge, and up the street facing us, we occupying an irregular position. When they got within sixty or seventy yards, Captain Brown said, "Let go upon them!" which we did, when several of them fell. Again and again the dose was repeated.

There was now consternation among the troops. From marching in solid martial columns, they became scattered. Some hastened to seize upon and bear up the wounded and dying—several lay dead upon the ground. They seemed not to realize, at first, that we would fire upon them, but evidently expected we would be driven out by them without firing.

Captain Brown seemed fully to understand the matter, and hence, very properly and in our defence, undertook to forestall their movements. The consequence of their unexpected reception was, after leaving several of their dead on the field, they beat a confused retreat into the bridge, and there stayed under cover until reinforcements came to the Ferry.

On the retreat of the troops, we were ordered back to our former post. While going, Dangerfield Newby, one of our colored men, was shot through the head by a person who took aim at him from a brick store window, on the opposite side of the street, and who was there for the purpose of firing upon us.

Newby was a brave fellow. He was one of my comrades at the Arsenal. He fell at my side, and his death was promptly avenged by Shields and Green, the Zouave of the band, who afterwards met his fate calmly on the gallows, with John Copeland.

Newby was shot twice; at the first fire, he fell on his side and returned it; as he lay, a second shot was fired, and the ball entered his head. Green raised his rifle in an instant, and brought down the cowardly murderer, before the latter could get his gun back through the sash.

There was comparative quiet for a time, except that the citizens seemed to be wild with terror. Men, women and children forsook the place in great haste, climbing up hillsides and scaling the mountains. The latter seemed to be alive with white fugitives, fleeing from their doomed city.

During this time, Wm. Thompson, who was returning from his errand to the Kennedy Farm, was surrounded on the bridge by the railroad men, who next came up, taken a prisoner to the Wager House, tied hand and foot, and, at a late hour of the afternoon, cruelly murdered by being riddled with balls, and thrown headlong on the rocks.

Late in the morning, some of his prisoners told Captain Brown that they would like to have breakfast, when he sent word forthwith to the Wager House to that effect, and they were supplied. He did not order breakfast for himself and men, as was currently but falsely stated at the time, as he suspected foul play; on the contrary, when solicited to have breakfast so provided for him, he refused.

Between two and three o'clock in the afternoon, armed men could be seen coming from every direction; soldiers were marching and counter-marching; and on the mountains, a host of blood-thirsty ruffians swarmed, waiting for their opportunity to pounce upon the little band.

The fighting commenced in earnest after the arrival of fresh troops. Volley upon volley was discharged, and the echoes from the hills, the shrieks of the townspeople, and the groans of their wounded and dying, all of which filled the air, were truly frightful. The Virginians may well conceal their losses, and Southern chivalry may hide its brazen head, for their boasted bravery was well tested that day, and in no way to their advantage.

It is remarkable, that except that one fool-hardy colored man was reported buried, no other funeral is mentioned, although the Mayor and other citizens are known to have fallen. Had they reported the true number, their disgrace would have been more apparent; so they wisely (?) concluded to be silent.

The fight at Harper's Ferry also disproved the current idea that slaveholders will lay down their lives for their property. Colonel Washington, the representative of the old hero, stood "blubbering" like a great calf at supposed danger; while the laboring white classes and non-slaveholders, with the marines (mostly gentlemen from "furrin" parts), were the men who faced the bullets of John Brown and his men. Hardly the skin of a slaveholder could be scratched in open fight; the cowards kept out of the way until danger was passed, sending the poor whites into the pitfalls, while they were reserved for the bragging, and to do the safe but cowardly judicial murdering afterwards.

As strangers poured in, the enemy took positions round about, so as to prevent any escape, within shooting distance of the engine house and Arsenal. Captain Brown, seeing their maneuvers, said: "We will hold on to our three positions, if they are unwilling to come to terms, and die like men."

All this time, the fight was progressing; no powder and ball were wasted. We shot from under cover, and took deadly aim. For an hour before the flag of truce was sent out, the firing was uninterrupted, and one and another of the enemy were constantly dropping to the earth.

One of the Captain's plans was to keep up communication between his three points. In carrying out this idea, Jerry Anderson went to the rifle factory, to see Kagi and his men. Kagi, fearing that we would be overpowered by numbers if the Captain delayed leaving, sent word by Anderson to advise him to leave the town at once. This word Anderson communicated to the Captain, and told us also at the Arsenal.

The message sent back to Kagi was, to hold out for a few minutes longer, when we would all evacuate the place. Those few minutes proved disastrous, for then it was that the troops before spoken of came pouring in, increased by crowds of men from the surrounding country.

After an hour's fighting, and when the enemy were blocking up the avenues of escape, Captain Brown sent out his son Watson with a flag of truce, but no respect was paid to it; he was fired upon, and wounded severely. He returned to the engine house, and fought bravely after that for fully an hour and a half, when he received a mortal wound, which he struggled under until the next day.

The contemptible and savage manner in which the flag of truce had been received, induced severe measures in our defence, in the hour and a half before the next one was sent out. The effect of our work was, that the troops ceased to fire at the buildings, as we clearly had the advantage of position.

Captain A.D. Stevens was next sent out with a flag, with what success I will presently show. Meantime, Jeremiah Anderson, who had brought the message from Kagi previously, was sent by Captain Brown with another message to John Henrie, but before he got far on the street, he was fired upon and wounded. He returned at once to the engine house, where he survived but a short time. The ball, it was found, had entered the right side in such manner that death necessarily ensued speedily.

Captain Stevens was fired upon several times while carrying his flag of truce, and received severe wounds, as I was informed that day, not being myself in a position to see him after. He was captured, and taken to the Wager House, where he was kept until the close of the struggle in the evening, when he was placed with the rest of our party who had been captured.

After the capture of Stevens, desperate fighting was done by both sides. The marines forced their way inside the engine-house yard, and commanded Captain Brown to surrender, which he refused to do, but said in reply, that he was willing to fight them if they would allow him first to withdraw his men to the second lock on the Maryland side.

As might be expected, the cowardly hordes refused to entertain such a proposition, but continued their assault, to cut off communication between our several parties.

The men at the Kennedy Farm having received such a favorable message in the early part of the day, through Thompson, were ignorant of the disastrous state of affairs later in the day. Could they have known the truth, and come down in time, the result would have been very different; we should not have been captured that day.

A handful of determined men, as they were, by taking a position on the Maryland side, when the troops made their attack and retreated to the bridge for shelter, would have placed the enemy between two fires. Thompson's news prevented them from hurrying down, as they otherwise would have done, and thus deprived us of able assistance from Owen Brown, a host in himself, and Tidd, Merriam and Coppic, the brave fellows composing that band.

The climax of murderous assaults on that memorable day was the final capture of the engine house, with the old Captain and his handful of associates. This outrageous burlesque upon civilized warfare must have a special chapter to itself, as it concentrates more of Southern littleness and cowardice than is often believed to be true.

CHAPTER XIII

The Capture of Captain John Brown at the Engine House

One great difference between savages and civilized nations is, the improved mode of warfare adopted by the latter. Flags of truce are always entitled to consideration, and an attacking party would make a wide departure from military usage, were they not to give opportunity for the besieged to capitulate, or to surrender at discretion.

Looking at the Harper's Ferry combat in the light of civilized usage, even where one side might be regarded as insurrectionary, the brutal treatment of Captain Brown and his men in the charge by the marines on the engine house is deserving of severest condemnation, and is one of those blood-thirsty occurrences, dark enough on depravity to disgrace a century.

Captain Hazlett and myself being in the Arsenal opposite, saw the charge upon the engine house with the ladder, which resulted in opening the doors to the marines, and finally in Brown's capture. The old hero and his men were hacked and wounded with indecent rage, and at last brought out of the house and laid prostrate upon the ground, mangled and bleeding as they were.

A formal surrender was required of Captain Brown, which he refused, knowing how little favor he would receive, if unarmed, at the hands of that infuriated mob.

All of our party who went from the Farm, save the Captain, Shields Green, Edwin Coppic and Watson Brown (who had received a mortal wound some time before), the men at the Farm, and Hazlett and I, were either dead or captured before this time; the particulars of whose fate we learned still later in the day, as I shall presently show.

Of the four prisoners taken at the engine house, Shields Green, the most inexorable of all our party, a very Turco in his hatred against the stealers of men, was under Captain Hazlett, and consequently of our little band at the Arsenal; but when we were ordered by Captain Brown to return to our positions, after having driven the troops into the bridge, he mistook the order, and went to the engine house instead of with his own party.

Had he remained with us, he might have eluded the vigilant Virginians. As it was, he was doomed, as is well-known, and became a freewill offering for freedom, with his comrade, John Copeland. Wiser and better men no doubt there were, but a braver man never lived than Shields Green.

CHAPTER XIV

Setting Forth Reasons Why O.P. Anderson and A. Hazlett Escaped from the Arsenal, Instead of Remaining, When They Had Nothing to Do—Took a Prisoner, and What Resulted to Them, and to This Narrative Therefrom—A Pursuit, When Somebody Got Killed, and Other Bodies Wounded

Of the six men assigned a position in the arsenal by Captain Brown, four were either slain or captured; and Hazlett and myself, the only ones remaining, never left our position until we saw with feeling of intense sadness, that we could be of no further avail to our commander, he being a prisoner in the hands of the Virginians.

We therefore, upon consultation, concluded it was better to retreat while it was possible, as our work for the day was clearly finished, and, gain a position where in the future we could work with better success, than to recklessly invite capture and brutality at the hands of our enemies. The charge of deserting our brave old leader and of fleeing from danger has been circulated to our detriment, but I have the consolation of knowing that, reckless as were the half-civilized hordes against whom we contended the entire day, and much as they might wish to disparage his men, they would never have thus charged us. They know better.

John Brown's men at Harper's Ferry were and are a unit in their devotion to John Brown and the cause he espoused. To have deserted him would have been to belie every manly characteristic for which Albert Hazlett, at least, was known by the party to be distinguished, at the same time that it would have endangered the future safety of such deserter or deserters.

John Brown gave orders; those orders must be obeyed, so long as Captain Brown was in a position to enforce them; once unable to command, from death, being a prisoner, or otherwise, the command devolved upon John Henry Kagi. Before Captain Brown was made prisoner, Captain Kagi had ceased to live, although had he been living, all communication between our post and him had been long cut off.

We could not aid Captain Brown by remaining. We might, by joining the men at the Farm, devise plans for his succor; or our experience might become available on some future occasion.

The charge of running away from danger could only find form in the mind of some one unwilling to encounter the difficulties of a Harper's Ferry campaign, as no one acquainted with the out-of-door and in-door encounters of that day will charge anyone with wishing to escape danger, merely.

It is well enough for men out of danger, and who could not be induced to run the risk of a scratching, to talk flippantly about cowardice, and to sit in judgment upon the men who went with John Brown, and who did not fall into the hands of the Virginians; but to have been there, fought there, and to understand what did transpire there, are quite different.

As Captain Brown had all the prisoners with him, the whole force of the enemy was concentrated there, for a time, after the capture of the rifle factory. Having captured our commander, we knew that it was but little two of us could do against so many, and that our turn to be taken must come; so Hazlett and I went out at the back part of the building, climbed up the wall, and went upon the railway.

Behind us, in the Arsenal, were thousands of dollars, we knew full well, but that wealth had no charms for us, and we hastened to communicate with the men sent to the Kennedy Farm.

We traveled up the Shenandoah along the railroad, and overtook one of the citizens. He was armed, and had been in the fight in the afternoon. We took him prisoner, in order to facilitate our escape. He submitted without resistance, and quietly gave up his gun.

From him, we learned substantially of the final struggle at the rifle factory, where the noble Kagi commanded. The number of citizens killed was, according to his opinion, much larger than either Hazlett or I had supposed, although we knew there were a great many killed and wounded together. He said there *must* be at least seventy killed, besides wounded. Hazlett has said there *must* be fifty, taken into account the defence of the three strong positions.

I do not know positively, but would not put the figure below thirty killed, seeing many fall as I did, and knowing the "dead aim" principle upon which we defended ourselves.

One of the Southern published accounts, it will be remembered, said twenty citizens were killed, another said fifteen. At last it got narrowed down to five, which was simply absurd, after so long an engagement.

We had forty rounds apiece when we went to the Ferry, and when Hazlett and I left, we had not more than twenty rounds between us. The rest of the party were as free with their ammunition as we were, if not more so. We had further evidence that the number of dead was larger than published, from the many that we saw lying dead around.

When we had gone as far as the foot of the mountains, our prisoner begged us not to take his life, but to let him go at liberty. He said we might keep his gun; he would not inform on us. Feeling compassion for him, and trusting to his honor, we suffered him to go, when he went directly into town, and finding every thing there in the hands of our enemies, he informed on us, and we were pursued.

After he had left us, we crawled or climbed up among the rocks in the mountains, some hundred yards or more from the spot where we left him, and hid ourselves, as we feared treachery, on second thought. A few minutes before dark, the troops came in search of us. They came to the foot of the mountains, marched and counter-marched, but never attempted to search the mountains; we supposed from their movements that they feared a host of armed enemies in concealment.

Their air was so defiant, and their errand so distasteful to us, that we concluded to apply a little ammunition to their case, and having a few cartridges on hand, we poured from our excellent position in the rocky wilds, some well-directed shots. It was not so dark but that we could see one bite the dust now and then, when others would run to aid them instantly, particularly the wounded. Some lay where they fell, undisturbed, which satisfied us that they were dead.

The troops returned our fire, but it was random shooting, as we were concealed from their sight by the rocks and bushes. Interchanging of shots continued for some minutes, with much spirit, when it became dark, and they went down into the town. After their return to the Ferry, we could hear the drum beating for a long time; an indication of their triumph, we supposed. Hazlett and I remained in our position three hours, before we dared venture down.

CHAPTER XV

The Encounter at the Rifle Factory

As stated in a previous chapter, the command of the rifle factory was given to Captain Kagi. Under him were John Copeland, Sherrard Lewis Leary, and three colored men from the neighborhood.

At an early hour, Kagi saw from his position the danger in remaining, with our small company, until assistance could come to the inhabitants. Hence his suggestion to Captain Brown, through Jeremiah Anderson, to leave.

His position being more isolated than the others, was the first to invite an organized attack with success; the Virginians first investing the factory with their hordes, before the final success at the engine house.

From the prisoner taken by us who had participated in the assault upon Kagi's position, we received the sad details of the slaughter of our brave companions. Seven different times during the day they were fired upon, while they occupied the interior part of the building, the insurgents defending themselves with great courage, killing and wounding with fatal precision.

At last, overwhelming numbers, as many as five hundred, our informant told us, blocked up the front of the building, battered the doors down, and forced their way into the interior. The insurgents were then forced to retreat the back way, fighting, however, all the time. They were pursued, when they took to the river, and it being so shallow, they waded out to a rock, mid-way, and there made a stand, being completely hemmed in, front and rear.

Some four or five hundred shots, said our prisoner, were fired at them before they were conquered. They would not surrender into the hands of the enemy, but kept on fighting until every one was killed, except John Copeland. Seeing he could do no more, and that all his associates were murdered, he suffered himself to be captured. The party at the rifle factory fought desperately till the last, from their perch on the rock. Slave and free, black and white, carried out the special injunction of the brave old Captain, to make sure work of it.

The unfortunate targets for so many bullets from the enemy, some of them received two or three balls. There fell poor Kagi, the friend and adviser of Captain Brown in his most trying positions, and the cleverest man in the party; and there also fell Sherrard Lewis Leary, generous-hearted and companionable as he was, and in that and other difficult positions, brave to desperation. There fought John Copeland, who met his fate like a man. But they were all "honorable men," noble, noble fellows who fought and died for the most holy principles.

John Copeland was taken to the guardhouse, where the other prisoners afterwards were, and thence to Charlestown jail. His subsequent mockery of a trial, sentence and execution, with his companion Shields Green, on the 16th of December—are they not part of the dark deeds of this era, which will assign their perpetrators to infamy, and cause after generations to blush at the remembrance?

CHAPTER XVI

Our Escape from Virginia—Hazlett Breaks down from Fatigue and Hunger—
Narrow Escape in Pennsylvania

I have said elsewhere, that Hazlett and I crossed over to the Maryland side, after the skirmish with the troops about nightfall. To be more circumstantial: When we descended from the rocks, we passed through the back part of the Ferry on the hill, down to the railroad, proceeding as far as the saw-mill on the Virginia side, where we came upon an old boat tied up to shore, which we cast off, and crossed the Potomac.

The Maryland shore once gained, we passed along the towpath of the canal for some distance when we came to an arch, which led through under the canal, and thence to the Kennedy Farm, hoping to find something to eat, and to meet the men who had been stationed on that side.

When we reached the farmhouse, all our expectations were disappointed. The old house had been ransacked and deserted, the provisions taken away, with everything of value to the insurgents. Thinking that we should fare better at the schoolhouse, we bent our steps in that direction, The night was dark and rainy, and after tramping for an hour and a half, at least, we came up to the schoolhouse. This was about two o'clock in the morning.

The schoolhouse was packed with things moved there by the party the previous day, but we searched in vain, after lighting a match, for food, our greatest necessity, or for our young companions in the struggle. Thinking it unsafe to remain in the schoolhouse, from fear of oversleeping ourselves, we climbed up the mountain in the rear of it, to lie down till daylight.

It was after sunrise some time when we awoke in the morning. The first sound we heard was shooting at the Ferry. Hazlett thought it must be Owen Brown and his men trying to force their way into the town, as they had been informed that a number of us had been taken prisoners, and we started down along the ridge to join them. When we got in sight of the Ferry, we saw the troops firing across the river to the Maryland side with considerable spirit.

Looking closely, we saw, to our surprise, that they were firing upon a few of the colored men, who had been armed the day before by our men, at the Kennedy Farm, and stationed down at the school-house by C. P. Tidd. They were in the bushes on the edge of the mountains, dodging about, occasionally exposing themselves to the enemy. The troops crossed the bridge in pursuit of them, but they retreated in different directions. Being further in the mountains, and more secure, we could see without personal harm befalling us.

One of the colored men came towards where we were, when we hailed him, and inquired the particulars. He said that one of his comrades had been shot, and was lying on the side of the mountains; that they thought the men who had armed them the day before must be in the Ferry. That opinion, we told him, was not correct. We asked him to join with us in hunting up the rest of the party, but he declined, and went his way.

While we were in this part of the mountains, some of the troops went to the schoolhouse, and took possession of it. On our return along up the ridge, from our position, screened by the bushes, we could see them as they invested it. Our last hope of shelter, or of meeting our companions, now being destroyed, we concluded to make our escape North.

We started at once, and wended our way along until dark, without being fortunate enough to overtake our friends, or to get anything to eat. As may be supposed, from such incessant activity, and not having tasted a morsel for forty-eight hours, our appetites were exceedingly keen. So hungry were we, that we sought out a cornfield, under cover of the night, gathered some of the ears—which, by the way, were pretty well hardened—carried them into the mountains—our fortunate resource—and, having matches, struck fire, and roasted and feasted.

During our perilous and fatiguing journey to Pennsylvania, and for some time after crossing the line, our only food was corn roasted in the ear, often difficult to get without risk, and seldom eaten but at long intervals. As a result of this poor diet and the hard journey, we became nearly famished, and very much reduced in bodily strength.

Poor Hazlett could not bear the privations as I could; he was less inured to physical exertion, and was of rather slight form, though inclined to be tall. With his feet blistered and sore, he held out as long as he could, but at last gave out, completely broke down, ten miles below Chambersburg. He declared it was impossible for him to go further, and begged me to go on, as we should be more in danger if seen together in the vicinity of the towns. He said, after resting that night, he would throw away his rifle, and go to Chambersburg in the stage next morning, where we agreed to meet again.

The poor young man's face was wet with tears when we parted. I was loath to leave him, as we both knew that danger was more imminent than when in the mountains around Harper's Ferry. At the latter place, the ignorant slaveholding aristocracy were unacquainted with the topography of their own grand hills; —in Pennsylvania, the cupidity of the pro-slavery classes would induce them to seize a stranger on suspicion, or to go hunting for our party, so tempting to them is the bribe offered by the Slave Power. Their debasement in that respect was another reason why we felt the importance of travelling at night, as much as possible.

After leaving young Hazlett, I traveled on as fast as my disabled condition would admit of, and got into Chambersburg about two hours after midnight. I went cautiously, as I thought, to the house of an acquaintance, who arose and let me in. Before knocking, however, I hid my rifle a little distance from the house.

My appearance caused my friend to become greatly agitated. Having been suspected of complicity in the outbreak, although he was in ignorance of it until it happened, he was afraid that, should my whereabouts become known to the United States Marshal, he would get into serious difficulty.

From him I learned that the Marshal was looking for Cook, and that it was not only unsafe for me to remain an hour, but that any one they chose to suspect would be arrested. I represented to him my famished condition, and told him I would leave as soon as I should be able to eat a morsel.

After having despatched my hasty meal, and while I was busy filling my pockets with bread and meat, in the back part of the house, the United States Marshal knocked at the front door. I stepped out at the back door to be ready for flight, and while standing there, I heard the officer say to my friend, "You are suspected of harboring persons who were engaged in the Harper's Ferry outbreak." A warrant was then produced, and they said they must search the house. These Federal hounds were watching the house, and supposing that whoever had entered was lying down, they expected to pounce upon their prey easily.

Hearing what I did, I started quietly away to the place where I left my arms, gathered them up, and concluded to travel as far as I could before daylight. When morning came, I went off the road some distance to where there was a straw stack, where I remained throughout the day.

At night, I set out and reached York, where a good Samaritan gave me oil, wine and raiment. From York, I wended my way to the Pennsylvania railroad. I took the train at night, at a convenient station, and went to Philadelphia, where great kindness was extended to me; and from there I came to Canada, without mishap or incident of importance.

To avoid detection when making my escape, I was obliged to change my apparel three times, and my journey over the railway was at first in the night-time, I lying in concealment in the day-time.

CHAPTER XVII

A Word or Two More about Albert Hazlett

I left Lieutenant Hazlett prostrate with fatigue and hunger, the night on which I went to Chambersburg. The next day, he went into the town, carrying his blanket, rifle and revolver, and proceeded to the house where Kagi had boarded.

The reward was then out for John E. Cook's arrest, and suspecting him to be Cook, Hazlett was pursued. He was chased from the house where he was by the officers, dropping his rifle in his flight. When he got to Carlisle, so far from receiving kindness from the citizens of his native State—he was from Northern Pennsylvania—he was arrested and lodged in jail, given up to the authorities of Virginia, and shamefully executed by them—his identity, however, never having been proven before the Court. A report of his arrest at the time reads as follows:

> The man arrested on suspicion of being concerned in the insurrection was brought before Judge Graham on a writ of habeas corpus today. Judge Watts presented a warrant from Governor Packer, of Pennsylvania, upon a requisition from the Governor of Virginia for the delivery of the fugitive named Albert Hazlett. There was no positive evidence to identify the prisoner.

Hazlett was remanded to the custody of the Sheriff. The Judge appointed a further hearing, and issued subpoenas for witnesses from Virginia, &c. No positive evidence in that last hearing was adduced, and yet Governor Packer ordered him to be delivered up; and the pro-slavery authorities made haste to carry out the mandate.

CHAPTER XVIII

Captain Owen Brown, Charles P. Tidd, Barclay Coppic, F. J. Merriam, John E. Cook

In order to have a proper understanding of the work done at Harper's Ferry, I will repeat, in a measure, separately, information concerning the movements of Captain O. Brown and company, given in connection with other matter.

This portion of John Brown's men was sent to the Maryland side previous to the battle, except Charles P. Tidd and John E. Cook, who went with our party to the Ferry on Sunday evening. These two were of the company who took Colonel Washington prisoner, but on Monday morning, they were ordered to the Kennedy Farm, to assist in moving and guarding arms.

Having heard, through some means, that the conflict was against the insurgents, they provided themselves with food, blankets, and other necessaries, and then took to the mountains. They were fourteen days making the journey to Chambersburg.

The weather was extremely bad the whole time; it rained, snowed, blew, and was freezing cold; but there was no shelter for the fugitive travelers, one of whom, F.J. Merriam, was in poor health, lame, and physically slightly formed. He was, however, greatly relieved by his companions, who did everything possible to lessen the fatigue of the journey for him. The bad weather, and their destitution, made it one of the most trying journeys it is possible for men to perform. Sometimes they would have to lie over a day or two for the sick, and when fording streams, as they had to do, they carried the sick over on their shoulders.

They were a brave band, and any attempt to arrest them in a body would have been a most serious undertaking, as all were well armed, could have fired some forty rounds apiece, and would have done it, without any doubt whatever. The success of the Federal officers consisted in arresting those unfortunate enough to fall into their clutches singly. In this manner did poor Hazlett and John E. Cook fall into their power.

Starvation several times stared Owen Brown's party in the face. They would search their pockets over and over for some stray crumb that might have been overlooked in the general search, for something to appease their gnawing hunger, and pick out carefully, from among the accumulated dirt and medley, even the smallest crumb, and give it to the comrade least able to endure the long and biting fast.

John E. Cook became completely overcome by this hungry feeling. A strong desire to get salt pork took possession of him, and against the remonstrances of his comrades, he ventured down from the mountains to Montaldo, a settlement fourteen miles from Chambersburg, in quest of it.

He was arrested by Daniel Logan and Clegget Fitzhugh, and taken before Justice Reisher. Upon examination, a commission signed by Captain Brown, marked No. 4, being found upon his person, he was committed to await a requisition from Governor Wise, and finally, as is well-known, was surrendered to Virginia, where he was tried, after a fashion, condemned, and executed.

It is not my intention to dwell upon the failings of John E. Cook. That he departed from the record, as familiar to John Brown and his men, every one of them "posted" in the details of their obligations and duties, well-knows; but his very weakness should excite our compassion. He was brave—none could doubt that, and life was invested with charms for him, which his new relation as a man of family tended to intensify; and charity suggests that the hope of escaping his merciless persecutors, and of being spared to his friends and associates in reform, rather than treachery to the cause he had espoused, furnishes the explanation of his peculiar sayings.

Owen Brown, and the other members of the party, becoming impatient at Cook's prolonged absence, began to suspect something was wrong, and moved at once to a more retired and safer position. Afterwards, they went to Chambersburg, and stopped in the outskirts of the town for some days, communicating with but one person, directly, while there. Through revelations made by Cook, it became unsafe in the neighborhood, and they left, and went some miles from town, when Merriam took the cars for Philadelphia; thence to Boston, and subsequently to Canada.

The other three traveled on foot to Centre County, Pennsylvania, when Barclay Coppic separated from them, to take the cars, with the rifles of the company boxed up in his possession. He stopped at Salem, Ohio, a few days and then went to Cleveland, from Cleveland to Detroit, and over into Canada, where, after remaining for a time, he proceeded westward. Owen Brown and C.P. Tidd went to Ohio, where the former spent the winter. The latter, after a sojourn, proceeded to Massachusetts.

CHAPTER XIX

The Behavior of the Slaves—Captain Brown's Opinion

Of the various contradictory reports made by slaveholders and their satellites about the time of the Harper's Ferry conflict, none were more untruthful than those relating to the slaves. There was seemingly a studied attempt to enforce the belief that the slaves were cowardly, and that they were really more in favor of Virginia masters and slavery, than of their freedom.

As a party who had an intimate knowledge of the conduct of the colored men engaged, I am prepared to make an emphatic denial of the gross imputation against them. They were charged specially with being unreliable, with deserting Captain Brown the first opportunity, and going back to their masters; and with being so indifferent to the work of their salvation from the yoke, as to have to be forced into service by the Captain, contrary to their will.

On the Sunday evening of the outbreak, when we visited the plantations and acquainted the slaves with our purpose to effect their liberation, the greatest enthusiasm was manifested by them—joy and hilarity beamed from every countenance.

One old mother, white-haired from age, and borne down with the labors of many years in bonds, when told of the work in hand, replied: "God bless you! God bless you!" She then kissed the party at her house, and requested all to kneel, which we did, and she offered prayer to God for His blessing on the enterprise, and our success.

At the slaves' quarters, there was apparently a general jubilee, and they stepped forward manfully, without impressing or coaxing. In one case, only, was there any hesitation. A dark complexioned free-born man refused to take up arms. He showed the only want of confidence in the movement, and far less courage than any slave consulted about the plan. In fact, so far as I could learn, the free blacks in the South are less reliable than the slaves, and infinitely more fearful.

In Washington City, a party of free colored persons offered their services to the Mayor, to aid in suppressing our movement. Of the slaves who followed us to the Ferry, some were sent to help remove stores, and the others were drawn up in a circle around the engine-house, at one time, where they were, by Captain Brown's order, furnished by me with pikes, mostly, and acted as a guard to the prisoners to prevent their escape, which they did.

As in the war of the American Revolution, the first blood shed was a black man's, Crispus Attuck's, so at Harper's Ferry, the first blood shed by our party, after the arrival of the United States troops, was that of a slave.

In the beginning of the encounter, and before the troops had fairly emerged from the bridge, a slave was shot. I saw him fall. Phil, the slave who died in prison, with fear, as it was reported, was wounded at the Ferry, and died from the effects of it. Of the men shot on the rocks, when Kagi's party were compelled to take to the river, some were slaves, and they suffered death before they would desert their companions, and their bodies fell into the waves beneath.

Captain Brown, who was surprised and pleased by the promptitude with which they volunteered, and with their manly bearing at the scene of violence, remarked to me, on that Monday morning, that he was agreeably disappointed in the behavior of the slaves; for he did not expect one out of ten to be willing to fight.

The truth of the Harper's Ferry "raid," as it has been called, in regard to the part taken by the slaves, and the aid given by colored men generally, demonstrates clearly: First, that the conduct of the slaves is a strong guarantee of the weakness of the institution, should a favorable opportunity occur; and, secondly, that the colored people, as a body, were well represented by numbers, both in the fight, and in the number who suffered martyrdom afterward.

The first report of the number of "insurrectionists" killed was seventeen, which showed that several slaves were killed; for there were only ten of the men that belonged to the Kennedy Farm who lost their lives at the Ferry, namely: John Henri Kagi, Jerry Anderson, Watson Brown, Oliver Brown, Stewart Taylor, Adolphus Thompson, William Thompson, William Leeman, all eight whites, and Dangerfield Newby and Sherrard Lewis Leary, both colored. The rest reported dead, according to their own showing, were colored.

Captain Brown had but seventeen with him, belonging to the Farm, and when all was over, there were four besides himself taken to Charlestown, prisoners, viz: A.D. Stevens, Edwin Coppic, white; John A. Copeland and Shields Green, colored. It is plain to be seen from this, that there was a proper percentage of colored men killed at the Ferry, and executed at Charlestown. Of those that escaped from the fangs of the human bloodhounds of slavery, there were four whites, and one colored man, myself being the sole colored man of those at the Farm.

That hundreds of slaves were ready, and would have joined in the work, had Captain Brown's sympathies not been aroused in favor of the families of his prisoners, and that a very different result would have been seen, in consequence, there is no question.

There was abundant opportunity for him and the party to leave a place in which they held entire sway and possession, before the arrival of the troops. And so cowardly were the slaveholders, proper, that from Colonel Lewis Washington, the descendant of the Father of his Country, General George Washington, they were easily taken prisoners. They had not pluck enough to fight, nor to use the well-loaded arms in their possession, but were concerned rather in keeping a whole skin by parlaying, or in spilling cowardly tears, to excite pity, as did Colonel Washington, and in that way escape merited punishment.

No, the conduct of the slaves was beyond all praise; and could our brave old Captain have steeled his heart against the entreaties of his captives, or shut up the fountain of his sympathies against their families—could he, for the moment, have forgotten them, in the selfish thought of his own friends and kindred, or, by adhering to the original plan, have left the place, and thus looked forward to the prospective freedom of the slave—hundreds ready and waiting would have been armed before twenty-four hours had elapsed.

As it was, even the noble old man's mistakes were productive of great good, the fact of which the future historian will record, without the embarrassment attending its present narration. John Brown did not only capture and hold Harper's Ferry for twenty hours, but he held the whole South. He captured President Buchanan and his Cabinet, convulsed the whole country, killed Governor Wise, and dug the mine and laid the train which will eventually dissolve the union between Freedom and Slavery.

The rebound reveals the truth. So let it be!

Other titles available
from World View Forum:

Southern Populism and Black Labor, by Vince Copeland

The Blast Furnace Brothers, by Vince Copeland

Expanding Empire, by Vince Copeland

The Built-in U.S. War Drive, by Vince Copeland

Market Elections: How Democracy Serves the Rich, by Vince Copeland

The Klan and the Government, by Sam Marcy

High Tech, Low Pay, by Sam Marcy

Anatomy of the Economic Crisis, by Sam Marcy

Workfare Workers Organize, by Larry Holmes and Shelley Ettinger

The Feeding Trough, by Phil Wilayto

The Roots of Lesbian & Gay Oppression, by Bob McCubbin